19.00
75D

earth resources

THE PRENTICE-HALL FOUNDATIONS OF EARTH SCIENCE SERIES

A. Lee McAlester, Editor

STRUCTURE OF THE EARTH

S. P. Clark, Jr.

EARTH MATERIALS

W. G. Ernst

THE SURFACE OF THE EARTH

A. L. Bloom

EARTH RESOURCES, 3rd ed.

B. J. Skinner

GEOLOGIC TIME, 2nd ed.

D. L. Eicher

ANCIENT ENVIRONMENTS, 2nd ed.

L. F. Laporte

THE HISTORY OF THE EARTH'S CRUST

D. L. Eicher, A. L. McAlester, and M. L. Rottman

THE HISTORY OF LIFE, 2nd ed.

A. L. McAlester

OCEANS, 2nd ed.

K. K. Turekian

MAN AND THE OCEAN

B. J. Skinner and K. K. Turekian

ATMOSPHERES

R. M. Goody and J. C. G. Walker

WEATHER, 2nd ed.

L. J. Battan

THE SOLAR SYSTEM

J. A. Wood

earth
resources

third edition

BRIAN J. SKINNER

Yale University

PRENTICE-HALL, INC., *Englewood Cliffs, New Jersey 07632*

Library of Congress Cataloging-in-Publication Data

Skinner, Brian J., (date)
  Earth resources.

  Bibliography: p.
  Includes index.
  1. Mines and mineral resources. 2. Power
resources. 3. Water-supply. I. Title.
TN153.S56 1986   553   85-12425
ISBN 0-13-223090-9

Editorial/production supervision: Maria McColligan

Interior and cover design: Lee Cohen

Manufacturing buyer: John Hall

10 9 8 7 6 5 4 3 2 1

PRENTICE-HALL INTERNATIONAL (UK) LIMITED, *London*

PRENTICE-HALL OF AUSTRALIA PTY. LIMITED, *Sydney*

PRENTICE-HALL CANADA INC., *Toronto*

PRENTICE-HALL HISPANOAMERICANA, S.A., *Mexico*

PRENTICE-HALL OF INDIA PRIVATE LIMITED, *New Delhi*

PRENTICE-HALL OF JAPAN, INC., *Tokyo*

PRENTICE-HALL OF SOUTHEAST ASIA PTE. LTD., *Singapore*

EDITORA PRENTICE-HALL DO BRASIL, LTDA., *Rio de Janeiro*

WHITEHALL BOOKS LIMITED, *Wellington, New Zealand*

contents

introduction

Our entire society rests upon—and is dependent upon—our water, our land, our forests, and our minerals. How we use these resources influences our health, security, economy, and well-being. (John F. Kennedy, Message on National Resources; Congress, February 23, 1961.)

Resource is a word with many shades of meaning. It can be used to describe courage needed to face a personal crisis, wood to fuel a stove and heat a house for the winter, or finances to meet a sudden medical expense. The resources discussed in this book all share a common factor. They are all *natural resources,* which means that they are the material and energy supplies drawn from the earth—supplies such as food, building and clothing materials, fertilizers, metals, water, and geothermal power.

Every living species needs and uses natural resources. We, *Homo sapiens,* have learned to use, and now to depend on, a vast number of natural resources. In so doing, our species has changed the natural distribution of many other animal species and has drastically altered patterns of plant growth. The result is the form of controlled living we call *civilization.* We have managed to combat climatic extremes in order to breed more productive and durable plants, and have thereby vastly increased the earth's yield of palatable foods. As a consequence, we have expanded our occupation of the globe to its farthest reaches and have increased our numbers far beyond those that once were in stable balance with unmanipulated nature. But we seem to have backed ourselves into an uncomfortable corner. We don't have much freedom to choose anymore. Maintenance of the earth's huge population now depends on continuing supplies of natural resources: fertilizers to increase crop yields, water to drink and to irrigate crops, metals to build machines, fuels to energize

1

the machines, and myriad other materials. Are there really sufficient quantities to sustain a long-term, healthy society? Without continuing supplies of natural resources, civilized society must collapse and the population wither. As we have become conscious of the supply question in recent years, we seem to have overreacted. Suddenly, in 1983 and 1984, some materials such as oil and copper were overproduced, a market glut developed, and some resources have probably been used in a less effective way than they might have been.

Natural resources fall into two distinct categories. Resources that arise from the heat and light radiated by the sun are called *renewable resources.* Examples are the water that falls as rain, the energy of blowing winds, food, cotton and wool, wood from living plants, and animals. Each is renewable because each is continually replenished by radiant energy reaching the earth's surface from the sun. Even though we consume the crop each season, the larder is replenished the following year when a new crop grows. As long as the sun's rays warm the earth, this pattern of renewal will continue. But *mineral resources,* such as coal, oil, copper, iron, uranium, fertilizers, and gold, are formed so exceedingly slowly—millions of years for each crop—that they are, for all practical purposes, *nonrenewable resources.* They are one-crop resources, and the earth's supplies of these commodities are fixed. Most of the resources discussed in this book are mineral resources, and they are nonrenewable. A few renewable resources, such as hydroelectric power, solar energy, and water supplies are also discussed, because their use is similar to, and closely allied with, the use of mineral resources.

The kinds of resources, their distribution, their quantities, the amounts we use, and our dependence on them are among the topics covered in this book. There are, of course, many questions in addition to those concerned with the adequacy of supplies of nonrenewable mineral resources. For example, as technologically advanced countries come to depend increasingly on supplies from less developed countries, political questions arise. Within producing countries, there are questions concerning the use and misuse of land that is laid open during mining operations. Questions concerning the dispersal of waste products—pollution—also inevitably follow the intensive use of mineral resources. As fascinating and important as these economic, social, and political questions are, they can only be mentioned and cannot, in a short volume such as this, be accorded a full discussion.

Mineral resources have become essential ingredients for life. They are the building blocks of society. But are they sufficient to sustain a healthy future, and are they sufficiently accessible to allow easy exploitation? Empires have flourished because they controlled rich and easily exploited mineral resources, but they withered as those riches declined. Are the world's remaining resources so distributed that the historical pattern of power dependence on resource availability is a thing of the past, or is it still the key to the future? Questions such as these are very controversial and cannot yet be answered unambiguously. But the questions have been raised, and they must eventually be answered. We all know that mineral resources are not uniformly distributed. The supplies of some materials, such as oil, are quite limited, and it is clear that they cannot be consumed at present rates for even another century. Adjustments and changes are inevitable and will influence all of us. Choices will have to be made, and each of us, directly and indirectly, will have our say. We should face these future choices with as much understanding as possible. This book does not provide all the answers, but it can help each of us in reaching our future decisions.

The study of the abundance and distribution of the earth's resources is, in its more basic aspects, a branch of geology. But the study of resources is not just a branch of geology. It is a topic that involves each and every one of us. It is a starting point for study of the history of civilization and of our occupancy of the earth. It is also a starting point for any discussion concerning future occupancy of the earth. It is my hope, therefore, that everyone will find topics of interest and food for thought within the pages of this book.

one

resources:
what they are and
where they are found

But the needed materials which can be recovered by known methods at reasonable cost from the earth's crust are limited, whereas their rates of exploitation and use obviously are not. (Walter R. Hibbard, Jr., in "Mineral Resources, Challenge or Threat?" Science, v. 160, p. 143, 1968.)

RESOURCES AND POPULATION

The human body is an engine fueled by food. Unfortunately, our bodies are not very efficient engines compared to internal combustion and steam engines. For example, if a healthy, hard-working man or woman rode an exercise cycle that in turn drove a small electrical generator, the best he or she could do during a full day of work would be to keep a single 100-watt light bulb burning. Human muscle power is really rather puny, and its limitations were all too evident to our ancestors. In order to keep their communities alive and healthy, to plow fields, till crops, build dams, and construct temples, our ancestors had to find ways to supplement their muscle power. First they domesticated beasts of burden; in the course of time, they learned to use sails, waterwheels, windmills, steam and internal combustion engines, and electric motors.

Supplementary sources of energy now exceed muscle energy in every part of our lives, from food production to recreation. Supplementary energy is like a gang of silent slaves who labor continually and uncomplainingly to feed, clothe, transport, and maintain us. The energy comes, of course, from the sun and from mineral resources such as coal, oil, and uranium, not from real slaves. But machines fueled by supplementary energy now rule our lives so completely that everyone on earth has "energy slaves" working for them. As the prices of oil, coal, and other fuels rise, we sometimes tend to forget how little it costs to purchase work equal to that of able-bodied men or women doing a full day of hard labor. The cost of the electricity needed to keep a 100-watt light bulb burning for 10 hours, is about 10 cents, and that cost includes the price of delivering the electricity through power lines, the cost of maintaining the power lines, and many other costs in addition to that of the fuel. If we consider just the cost of fuel, the figure is even more striking. If we were to purchase oil for $40 a barrel and ignore additional costs, such as those of distribution, the equivalent energy cost for a full day of work would drop to 1.5¢. Small wonder, then, that even in relatively poor countries such as India, the total amount of supplementary energy used by every man, woman, and child is equivalent to the work of 15 slaves, each working an eight-hour day. In South America everyone has approximately 30 "energy slaves," in Japan 100, Russia 120, Europe 150, and in the United States and Canada a huge 300. The concept of "energy slaves" demonstrates how utterly dependent the world has become on mineral resources. If the "slaves" were to strike (which means if the supplies ran out), the world's peoples could not keep themselves alive and healthy. Reverting to muscle power alone would bring starvation, famine, and pestilence. Nature would quickly reduce the population.

It would be misleading to dwell on energy alone. The use of all natural resources, renewable and nonrenewable, is intertwined. Oil is of little use unless we have engines built of iron, copper, lead, zinc, and other metals. Farmlands will only yield maximum crops if they are tilled by tractors and plows, and fertilized with compounds of phosphorus, nitrogen, and potassium. Figure 1-1 demonstrates dramatically how the yield of one of the world's basic food crops, corn, is influenced by the rate at which other resources are used to produce the crop.

How far can food production be pushed? The question is debatable but nevertheless vital. The basic question is one of rate—how much food can be produced in any growing season. We cannot consume renewable resources faster than we can grow them, and even though the farmers of the world managed to double the annual food production between 1960 and 1980, there is certainly a limit to the *rate* of food production. The limit is imposed by the size of the earth, the amount of sunlight falling on it, the way sunlight varies with latitude, and the efficiency with which plants can use the sunlight.

It is little appreciated that despite the so-called green revolution and the great advances in farming methods, gains in agricultural output since 1970 have barely kept pace with needs because of excessive population growth (Fig. 1-2). Today only a few countries in the world consistently produce sufficient food to keep their populations healthy. There are even fewer countries—the most important are Australia, Canada, New Zealand, South Africa, and the United States—that regularly produce food in excess of their own needs and

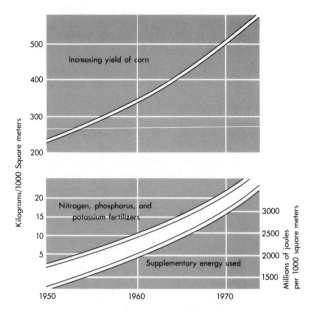

FIG. 1-1 Increased food requirements demand greater crop yields which in turn require increased inputs of mineral resources. In North America the average yield of corn per thousand square meters more than doubled between 1950 and 1970. Increased amounts of machinery, fertilizers, and energy were needed. The energy figures take into account such factors as the energy used in making tractors and in preparing fertilizers, insecticides, and herbicides. (After Pimental et al., 1973, *Science,* v. 182, p. 443.) By 1980 the average fertilizer addition in the United States had risen to more than double the 1970 figure, and in Japan and some European countries it had reached levels twice as high as those in the United States.

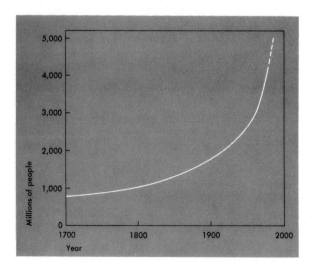

FIG. 1-2 Growth rate of the earth's human population.

are able to meet the imbalance for the rest of the world. The increase in population is the basic reason that so few countries have excess food to export.

Even with enormous efforts to expand production from all sources, including the oceans, it is obvious that present trends are not stable; it is inevitable, therefore, that the world population must eventually cease growing. We must hope that the world's population will soon attain a realistic size that can live in equilibrium with a stable rate of food production. The definition of this realistic size and the means of holding it in balance are probably the two greatest problems facing mankind today.

Balance and control of the size of the population will demand societal responsibilities beyond any that mankind has ever attained. But those responsibilities will not be faced until the controls that natural resources—and especially mineral resources—exert on population size, on production rates of resources, and on living standards are fully appreciated. Nor will the definition of a stable population be decided unless the earth's supply limitations are accurately assessed. As the reader of this book will discover, the assessment of resources is a very complex problem and one that remains to be solved. Relative abundances, though, are already known, and trends can be discerned. On the basis of such trends, some experts suggest that the stable population size has already been exceeded. If they are correct, we should already be reducing our population size. Other experts suggest that the limit has not yet been reached, but that it is less than twice the present world population.

There is a strong element of personal choice in all decisions regarding populations. The more people there are, the less there is to go around, and the lower the living standard will be. Individual countries or regions will have to decide what their stable populations will be, and indirectly, therefore, what their living standards will be. Thus, each of us will be involved in the most momentous decision our country has ever made. To commence our discussion of mineral resources, let us first consider what is meant by the statement that consumption rates are growing.

WHAT IS THE GROWTH RATE?

The consumption of almost all mineral resources is growing. When we examine the growth rate, we observe that, even though there are fluctuations due to economic and social upturns and downturns (Fig. 1-3), the overall rate of growth is not increasing by a constant amount each year, but rather the growth appears to be increasing by some percentage of the whole. The population growth curve in Fig. 1-2 is certainly not a straight line either. It also seems to be growing by some percentage of the whole each year, rather like compound interest. The mathematical term to describe curves such as those in Figs. 1-2 and 1-3 is *exponential functions,* and we refer to the growth they describe as *exponential growth.* Compound interest on a savings bank account is a familiar form of exponential growth. As any savings account holder knows

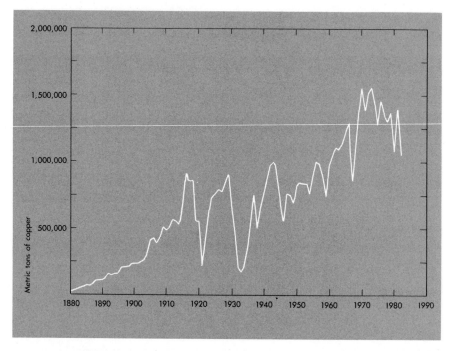

FIG. 1-3 Fluctuating production of copper in the United States. The overall trend is upward, but the curve is highly irregular because of short-term fluctuations due to factors such as economic recessions, wars, and industry strikes. (After U.S. Bureau of Mines.)

well, the amount paid in interest is a little larger each year, and, after a certain number of years, the size of the account will double. The *doubling time* depends, of course, on the interest rate.

It is self-evident that exponential growth cannot continue forever, so curves such as those in Figs. 1-2 and 1-3 must eventually change. Consider the case for population: According to demographers working for the United Nations, the world's population was growing at a rate of 1.7 percent a year at the end of 1982. At this rate, the world population will double in 41 years. Much of the present-day growth results from the fact that death rates have declined faster than birth rates have. In the less developed countries the speed with which the death rate is declining has now started to slow down [Fig. 1-4(A)]. This suggests to one expert, as shown in Fig. 1-4(B), that by the year 2100, the rate of population increase in today's less developed countries will have declined to zero. The population size in those countries will then be stable. That desirable state will be reached by today's developed countries at an earlier date than the year 2100, so we can hypothesize that the population curve will become sigmoidal in shape, and that in the future the world's population will level out to some constant value, as shown in the dashed projection in Fig. 1-4(A). Just what that constant value will be remains to be seen, so no

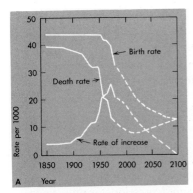

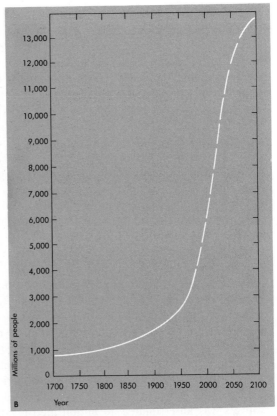

FIG. 1-4 Possible future projections for the world's population: (A) Birth rate and death rate in less developed countries of the world. The dashed portions of the curves are projections. When the birth rate and death rate are equal, in the year 2100, the rate of population increase will be zero. (After Ansley J. Coale, 1983 *Science*, v. 221, p. 828–832. (B) When the rate of population increase is zero around the world, the population curve will flatten out to a constant value as shown diagramatically by the dashed curve. The exact number at which the population will stabilize remains conjectural.

significance should be attached to the position of the dashed line. For the present the total population is still increasing and the world's population, which was 4.55 billion at the end of 1982, will rise to about 6 billion by the year 2000 and to about 10 billion by the year 2030.

The consumptions of many mineral resources are still growing at exponential rates. Furthermore, the growth rates of many mineral resources are faster than the rate of population growth. Use of gold, for example, increases at a rate of about 4 percent a year, corresponding to a doubling period of 18 years, while consumption of fertilizers has for years been growing at nearly 7 percent a year, and a doubling period of 10 years. When we examine these consumption figures more closely, we find two components to the growth rates of mineral resources. The first component clearly arises from increasing population—more people need products to support them. The second component is a measure of the rising standard of living around the world and of the increasingly complex technological underpinning of our society. It is possible to get a measure of the second component by dividing the annual gross consumption of a mineral product by a number equal to the population consuming the product; the result is a figure called *per capita consumption*. For a great many mineral products the per capita consumption curves have long been increasing exponentially. Total consumption curves, therefore, are the sum of the two separate exponential curves, and the population problem is a double-barreled one. Not only must the size eventually become stabilized, so too must living standards. When that time is reached, one unfortunate consequence of exponential consumption curves will be eased. The unfortunate consequence is that recycling can never satisfy the demands of exponential growth. No matter how efficiently a material is recycled, exponential growth demands that new material must continually be added from the earth's stock of nonrenewable resources.

To be sure that we are seeing exponential growth rate, and not just short-term fluctuations such as those caused by wars and depressions, we must conduct observations over a number of years. Observations over time spans of 50 years or more all point to the story illustrated in Fig. 1-5. Despite fluctuations, the consumption of most mineral resources on a worldwide basis continues to increase relentlessly. During 1980, per capita consumptions in the United States included 2.83 metric tons of sand and gravel, 3.9 metric tons of crushed stone, 42.4 kilograms of potash fertilizer, and 19.2 kilograms of aluminum. These figures highlight the most direful consequence of exponential growth. When the available stock is fixed in size, demand must ultimately exceed the ability of the stock to meet the rate of the demand, no matter how large the stock may be. Consider an absurd extreme: Throughout the present century, the world's annual production of mineral resources has approximately doubled every 10 years. In 1983, a period of economic downturn and reduced production, the world production of all kinds of new mineral resources was an estimated 30 billion metric tons. If a 10-year doubling time were maintained until the year 2213—that is, for 230 years—the people living then would have to produce 250,000,000 billion metric tons a year. This is absurd indeed; that mass is equal to all of the land standing above sea level.

Continued growth, whether exponential or not, cannot continue forever, and we must ask ourselves whether future consumption curves might look like the suggested population curve in Fig. 1-4(B). For a few resources, it is already possible to detect a flattening of consumption curves, especially in countries with high living standards. From such observations, experts predict an eventual levelling off of all natural resources to a constant per capita consumption rate. World consumption of mineral resources is still growing, however, and because industrialization and living standards are unevenly developed around the world, the geographic consumption of mineral resources is not uniform. As an example, compare the difference in per capita consumption during 1980 for certain mineral resources in the United States and in the world as a whole (Table 1-1). The figures for the United States are similar to those for most of the industrial countries of the world, which means that per capita consumption in the less developed or so-called third world countries, is very low. Simply raising the per capita consumption of all mineral resources, and the living standard, for the peoples of the third world to the rate presently enjoyed by

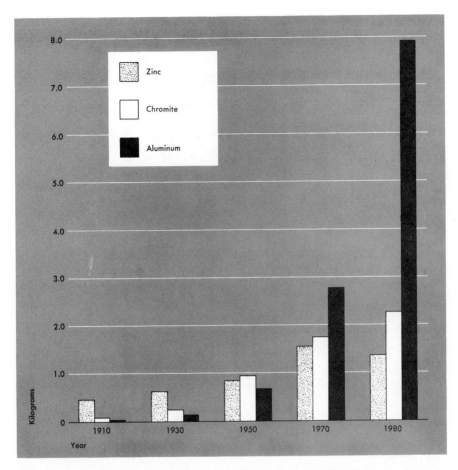

FIG. 1-5 Examples of per capita consumption, on a worldwide basis, for some representative mineral products. Chromite is a source of metallic chromium, a vital alloying metal in steels, and is also used for high temperature furnace linings and in preparing chemicals. Aluminum is used principally in the building, transportation, packaging, and electrical industries. Note that per capita consumption of zinc appears to be levelling off, while chromite and aluminum continue to grow exponentially. (After U.S. Bureau of Mines.)

the inhabitants of North America and Europe would tax the known supplies of many metals severely.

The geographic distribution of mineral resources on a worldwide basis is very uneven. Countries may be rich in one commodity but poor in another; no country is self-sufficient in all commodities, and it seems likely that no country will ever reach that state. The United States is self-sufficient in a very few commodities, including lead, molybdenum, and coal, while some commodities, such as tantalum and chromium, are entirely imported (Table 1-2). Production and consumption of mineral resources, therefore, raise complex

Table 1-1 Per capita consumptions of selected mineral commodities in the world and the United States in 1980. Large per capita consumptions are characteristic in industrially advanced countries.

Mineral Commodity	1980 PER CAPITA CONSUMPTION	
	World	United States
IRON AND STEEL	165 kilograms	272 kilograms
POTASH FERTILIZER	10.2	42.2
ALUMINUM	7.89	19.2
COPPER	3.71	8.62
NICKEL	0.18	0.59
TIN	0.057	0.21
TUNGSTEN	0.018	0.076
COBALT	0.007	0.031

(After U.S. Bureau of Mines).

questions of international trade and politics. If we are to meet both the world's aspirations for a high standard of living and for the maintenance of a large population, it is imperative that we appreciate and understand the nature and distribution of the resources that we must use.

Table 1-2 Percentage of selected mineral commodities that had to be imported into the United States during 1980.

Mineral Commodity	Percentages Imported	Main Supply Countries
CHROMIUM	100	South Africa, U.S.S.R., Turkey, Albania, the Philippines
TANTALUM	100	Australia, Canada, Zaire, Brazil, China
PLATINUM	99	South Africa, U.S.S.R., Canada
MANGANESE	95	Brazil, Gabon, South Africa, Australia
TIN	93	Malaysia, Thailand, Indonesia, Bolivia, Brazil
NICKEL	91	Canada, U.S.S.R., Botswana, Philippines
ASBESTOS	78	Canada, Mexico, Saudi Arabia
SILVER	75	Canada, Peru, Mexico, Australia
GOLD	70	South Africa, U.S.S.R., Canada
COPPER	30	Canada, Chile, Peru, Zambia, Zaire

(After U.S. Bureau of Mines).

KINDS OF MINERAL AND ENERGY RESOURCES

Throughout this book we shall use the term *mineral resources* in the most general sense. The term will be taken to include all nonliving, naturally occurring substances that are useful to us, whether they are inorganic or organic. By this definition, all natural solids, fossil fuels such as petroleum or natural gas, as well as the waters of the earth and gases of the atmosphere, are mineral resources. In addition to the mineral resources we use for energy—coal, oil, natural gas, uranium—there are many other sources of energy, both renewable and nonrenewable. We must consider sources such as water power and wind, which are renewable, and geothermal energy, which is largely nonrenewable. To help clarify the question of renewable versus nonrenewable, we shall classify the different types of resources discussed in this book on the basis of use, as demonstrated in Fig. 1-6.

It is instructive to compare the relative monetary values we place on different kinds of mineral resources. The value of mineral resources produced in the United States, divided into fuels, metals, and nonmetals (excluding water), is plotted in Fig. 1-7. Fuels accounted for 86 percent of the total value in 1982 and are clearly the leaders. The relative values of minerals consumed in all industrial countries are similar. Figure 1-7 demonstrates two important relationships discussed earlier. First, the overall value of natural resources con-

FIG. 1-6 Classification of mineral and energy resources. Shading indicates those energy resources that are not mineral resources.

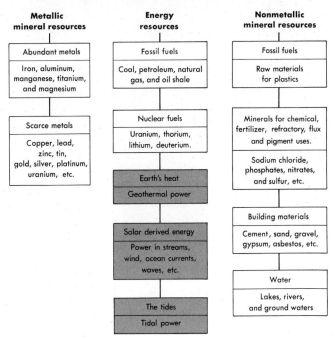

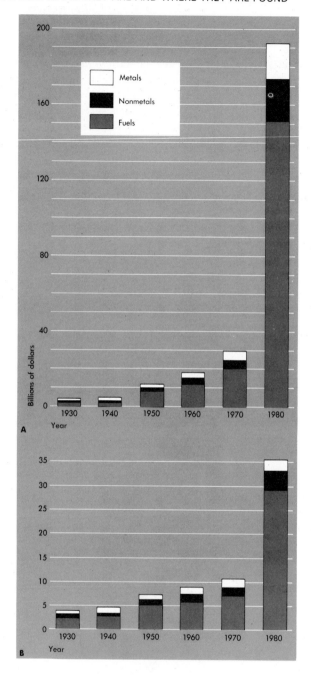

FIG. 1-7 Estimated value of annual mineral production in the United States. (After U.S. Bureau of Mines.) (A) Value in current dollars. (B) Value, corrected for inflation, in constant 1930 dollars.

sumed is increasing exponentially, reflecting exponential consumption rates. Second, increases in metals and nonmetals are parallel to the increase in fuels, reflecting the interdependence of all mineral resources.

A WORD ABOUT MEASUREMENT UNITS

We are all familiar with different ways of measuring volumes. For example, some things are usually measured by the cubic foot, others by the cubic centimeter; many liquid volumes are measured by the gallon or liter, wood is measured by the cord and the board foot, fruits and vegetables by the bushel, and oil and cement by the strangest unit of all, the barrel. A barrel of oil is equal to 42 U.S. gallons, while a barrel of cement, actually defined in terms of weight, is equal to 170.5 kilograms. The same kind of confusion reigns among units of weight, length, and energy, and in no field is the confusion more widespread than in the field of mineral resources. Fortunately, units are slowly being changed and standardized, but most mineral resources are still measured in archaic units that are sustained by custom rather than by reason.

To avoid the inconvenience of continually converting from one unit to another, the units used throughout this volume will be metric units. The units of length are the centimeter, meter, and kilometer; of volume, the cubic centimeter, cubic kilometer, and liter; of mass, the gram, kilogram, and metric ton; of energy, the joule; and of power, which measures the rate at which energy is produced or consumed, the watt. Conversion factors between these basic units and those commonly used in commerce and industry are given in Table A-1 of the Appendix. Perhaps the least familiar units for many readers are the metric ton and the joule. A metric ton is 1,000 kilograms and is equivalent to 2,204 pounds. To a first approximation, therefore, a metric ton can be equated with the common long ton of 2,240 pounds. A joule is a unit of energy used mainly in electricity, and is equal to 0.239 calorie. To a first approximation, therefore, 4 joules can be considered equivalent to a calorie.

RESOURCES VERSUS RESERVES

When a new copper deposit or a new oil field is discovered, one of the first questions asked is always, how much does it contain? Similarly, when the future of a mine is discussed, we ask, how much is left? But, how much of what? Do we mean material that can be profitably recovered today, or do we mean material that can only be recovered some time in the future, when prices are higher, or when a new recovery method has been invented? And how closely must the answer be estimated? To the nearest kilogram, to within 5 percent of the total, perhaps even to within 50 percent of the amount present?

The problem is particularly confusing where mineral resources are concerned because even though we use mineral commodities in every aspect of our daily lives, few among us have actually seen a mineral deposit or have any understanding of how one is formed, how big or small one is, and the difficulties involved in producing mineral raw materials. By contrast, we all have seen such renewable resources as cattle, corn fields, and apple trees and have a reasonable knowledge of the processes by which food is produced and of how it reaches our tables.

A *mineral resource* is any currently or potentially extractable concentration of naturally occurring solid, liquid, or gaseous material. Extraction must of course be profitable, so note the distinction drawn between currently and potentially extractable minerals. The term *mineral resource* has two components. The first, or currently extractable component, is an *identified resource,* or, as it is more commonly called, an *ore* or a *reserve.* We know how to exploit ores and the costs of their recovery. We can rely on them, and they can be profitably recovered today. The second, or potentially extractable component, is a *potential resource* that still has many ifs, ands, or buts attached to it. Perhaps new mining technology must be developed or new processing methods found, or perhaps government price supports are needed. Whatever the reasons, unanswered questions surround potential resources. Future developments are needed before they can become ores. But potential resources are materials that deserve special attention and that, for reasons of size, richness, or location, lead us to postulate that they might one day be used and become ores. The certainty with which we can guess the likelihood of potential resources ever becoming ores decreases the further we move from common experience, the more unconventional the materials we include in the estimate, and the further we project our guesses of economic and technological changes into the future.

There are many examples of potential resources becoming ores because of some special circumstance, but there have also been many times when ores have become too expensive to produce and have slipped back to become potential resources. It is all too easy in the course of a discussion of natural resources to forget that quite large concentrations of materials can, for one reason or another, be much too expensive to produce. There is not sufficient space in a short volume such as this to discuss the economics of each natural resource mentioned; you, the reader, must always keep in mind the fact that while natural resources are products of natural processes operating in the past, they become ores, and therefore reserves, only if we are smart enough to find a way to exploit them profitably. The preceding discussion emphasizes a point that should be clear but that is sometimes overlooked: We will always mine selectively, seeking out the richest, the most conveniently located, and the largest concentrations first. The occasional suggestion that we will soon turn to common rocks and seawater to recover most of our mineral resources, essentially ignoring the local concentrations that are ore deposits, seems highly improbable.

In all that has been said so far, we must also be aware of another ever-present factor that must be considered—the economic health of society. As this volume was being written in 1984, the world was struggling to recover from a period of severe economic downturn. This was a period when production of oil and metals such as copper and aluminum was so great that there were gluts on the market, and prices dropped markedly. If history is a reliable teacher, the gluts will disappear, prices will rise again, the recession will lift, and the upward trends of consumption will continue.

two

where mineral resources are found

. . . minerals . . . are formed in the earth's crust by infinitesimally slow natural geologic processes acting for thousands or millions of years. (D. A. Brobst and W. P. Pratt, U.S. Geological Survey, Professional Paper 820, 1973).

THE EARTH

Mineral resources are everywhere—in the atmosphere, the oceans, high in the mountains, in rocks beneath the seafloor, and indeed in every accessible region of the earth—but they are not uniformly distributed. On the contrary, they are very unevenly distributed, and they differ in kind and amount and from place to place. In order to put the distribution of resources in perspective, then, we should briefly examine some of the essential features of the planet on which we live.

Earth has a mass of 6×10^{21} metric tons and is comprised of 88[1] different chemical elements. The total tonnage of any element—even those present in extremely low concentrations—is truly enormous. Even though most of the earth is inaccessible and the tonnage that is actually within reach of the earth's surface is 5000 times less than the earth's total mass, the amount of any element down to 10 kilometers is still astronomically large. At the earth's center there is a metallic *core* consisting predominantly of iron and nickel; the core is surrounded by a *mantle* of dense rock rich in iron and magnesium:

---

[1]Uranium is element number 92, but four elements with lower atomic numbers have not been identified on earth. They may once have been here but have now disappeared through radioactive decay.

The core and mantle together account for more than 99.6 percent of the total mass of the earth. Above the mantle is the *crust,* which is the only portion of the solid earth that we actually observe. The crust accounts for 0.375 percent of the earth's mass. The crust consists of two parts: one that projects above the oceans and one that lies below. The portion above, in addition to a narrow sea-covered fringe around each continent, is called the *continental crust;* the portion below the oceans is the *oceanic crust* (Fig. 2-1).

Water in the oceans, lakes, and rivers, together with that trapped in holes and fractures in soil and near-surface rocks, is called the *hydrosphere,* and it accounts for 0.025 percent of the earth's mass. The gaseous *atmosphere,* which accounts for only 0.0001 percent of the mass, envelopes the whole earth. The upper portion of the crust, the hydrosphere and the atmosphere, are the regions where we find living plants and animals. The mass of living matter is called the *biosphere* and accounts for 0.0000003 percent of the earth's mass. It is from the four outermost and smallest zones—the crust, hydrosphere, biosphere, and atmosphere—that we draw our present resources and to which we must look for those of the future. The mantle and the core are so inaccessible that they cannot ever be seriously considered as potential suppliers of resources.

The Crust

Most mineral resources are derived from the crust. The crust obviously differs in important ways from the hydrosphere and atmosphere. First, it is

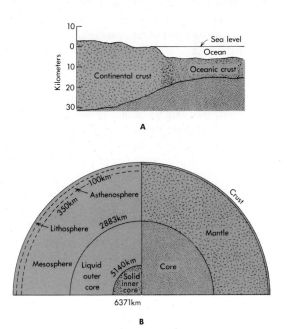

FIG. 2-1 Cross-section through the earth revealing the various layers. (A) The crust varies in thickness from place to place and has a distinctly different composition from that of the mantle below. The continental crust reaches thicknesses of 60 kilometers and averages about 30 kilometers. The oceanic crust is thinner— about 10 kilometers—and somewhat different in composition from the continental crust. (B) Major compositional layers in the earth shown on the right are the crust and mantle, both rocky, and the core, which is metallic. On the left are the layers with distinctly different physical properties; the lithosphere is rigid and brittle, the asthenosphere is ductile and easily deformed, and the mesosphere has properties intermediate between the lithosphere and asthenosphere.

predominantly composed of *minerals*—crystalline solids with specific and usually rather simple compositions. Second, as any walk through a rocky terrain will reveal, minerals are not randomly distributed, but are locally concentrated into specific and distinctive groupings called *rocks*. Limestone, for example, is a rock consisting mostly of the mineral calcite, $CaCO_3$. Granite consists largely of three minerals: potassium feldspar, $KAlSi_3O_8$; muscovite, $KAl_3Si_3O_{10}(OH)_2$; and quartz, SiO_2. Coal is a rock largely composed of solid organic matter. The chemical elements are therefore not evenly distributed through the crust but are distinctly segregated. Even elements that have a low *average* concentration in the crust are sometimes found in exceedingly high *local* concentrations. The richest local concentrations are *ore deposits*.

It is difficult to sample the floor of the ocean, but the composition of the oceanic crust is now reasonably well known. It consists largely of minerals rich in calcium, magnesium, iron, aluminum, and silicon that form by the cooling of lavas extruded on the sea floor to form a type of rock called *basalt*. The oceanic crust is largely a submarine phenomenon. Rarely, and only in special places, such as in Hawaii, Iceland, and other oceanic islands, is it elevated above sea level and subjected to the same forces of erosion that wear down the continents.

The continental crust contains somewhat more than half the mass of the entire crust, or approximately 0.29 percent of the earth's mass; it contains less iron, calcium, and magnesium than the oceanic crust, but relatively more silicon, aluminum, sodium, and potassium. The entire crust, oceanic and continental, plus the upper portion of the mantle, are called the *lithosphere,* which is a 100 kilometer thick zone of hard brittle rocks. The lithosphere seems to float, or to be buoyed up, on a plastic, almost liquidlike region of the mantle called the *asthenosphere* (Fig. 2-1). The floating property of the lithosphere helps explain why ocean basins are low and continents are elevated. Rocks of the oceanic crust are more dense than those of the continental crust. The continents float high, like blocks of light wood floating on water; oceanic crust sits lower, like blocks of heavy wood. There is, however, a little more water in the hydrosphere than the basins formed by the low-lying oceanic crust can contain. The oceans, therefore, spill over onto the continental margins, creating a submerged continental shelf and continental slope (Fig. 2-2). As we shall see, these submerged margins of continental crust have a potentially important role in the future of mineral resources.

A systematic examination of all known rock types shows that two principal kinds predominate. The first are *igneous* rocks, formed by the cooling and crystallization of liquids called *magmas* formed deep in the crust or upper part of the mantle. The second are *sedimentary rocks,* formed by compaction and cementation of sediment derived from the erosion of the continents by water, atmosphere, ice, and wind. Most of the sediments are deposited in low-lying depressions on the continents or in the sea along the margins of continents. As the marginal piles of sediment grow larger and are buried more

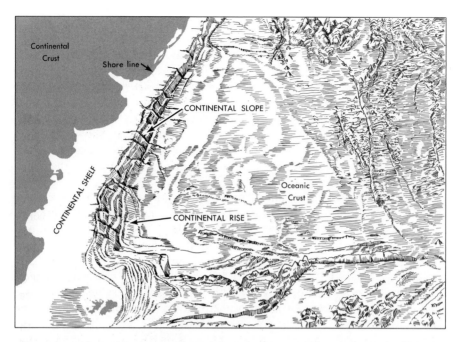

FIG. 2-2 Diagram of the edge of the South American continent off Argentina. The edge of the continental crust is marked by the steep continental slope. Seawater overlaps part of the continent to form the continental shelf. (After B. C. Heezen and M. Tharp, for the Geological Society of America.)

deeply, increasing pressure and rising temperature produce physical and chemical changes in them. Temperatures and pressures may also rise during mountain-building processes when moving continental crusts collide, squeeze, and change their marginal piles of sediment. The resulting *metamorphic rocks,* however, generally show whether they were originally sedimentary or igneous rocks. When the base of a compressed sedimentary pile is pushed deep enough, melting may start, and material near the bottom may melt to form magma. The newly formed magma, being liquid and less dense than the solid metamorphic rocks from which it was derived, will tend to rise up, intruding its parent; as it cools and crystallizes, it will form new igneous rock. Thus, there seem to be sequential processes whereby rocks of the continental crust are being continually reworked. The processes are slow—hundreds of millions of years are sometimes necessary—and the details are complicated, but they produce the chemical separations that lead to the chemical heterogeneity of the continental crust. As weathering and erosion occur, for example, some substances are dissolved and removed in solution, while others are transported as suspended particles. Extreme chemical separation can occur, and many of our mineral resources form as a result. It is an interesting discovery that the evolutionary processes that produced the atmosphere and hydrosphere which are so necessary for life on earth have also been essential for producing the chemical separations that are necessary for the formulation of some of the richest ores.

The continental crust contains an extremely varied array of rock types. It also contains a great deal of evidence to suggest that most of the rock-forming processes we can observe today have been active for at least 3,800 million years. Apparently, however, the continental crust, the atmosphere, and the waters of the hydrosphere have not always had the same composition.

The oceanic crust, in contrast to the continental crust, shows little variation in composition. This leads to the suspicion that the rocks below the seafloor do not contain the same diversity of mineral resources as the continental crust contains.

Scientists have long sought a single explanation for such diverse features as the compositional differences between oceanic and continental crust, the near parallelism of the coast lines on the two sides of the Atlantic Ocean, and the topography of mountain ranges, both on the ocean floor and on the land. A major advance in the search came during the 1960's, when it was finally proved that the outer 100 kilometers of the solid earth, the brittle lithosphere, slides slowly around on top of the plastic asthenosphere, rather like a loose skin, and that the sliding skin of lithosphere carries the continents with it. The analogy with a skin is only partly correct, because the lithosphere is actually broken into six huge fragments, or plates, plus a number of smaller ones (Fig. 2-3), and each plate moves more or less independently. New igneous rock forms

FIG. 2-3 A world map showing the major plates of lithosphere. Spreading edges are where magma wells up from the mantle to create new lithosphere; subduction edges are where lithosphere plunges down into the asthenosphere. Transform faults are plate boundaries along which two plates simply slide past each other.

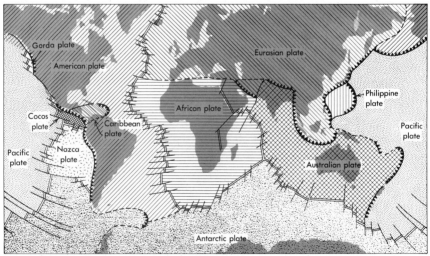

Plate boundaries

===== Spreading   ▲▲▲▲▲ Subduction   ——— Transform fault   – – – Uncertain

continually along giant fracture zones rending the ocean bottoms where two plates move away from each other. The rising basaltic magma helps to push the plates sideways. New oceanic crust is created by this process. Because the size of the earth is fixed, some other process must also destroy oceanic crust at the same rate new crust is formed. This occurs when the oldest portions of the moving plates cool down, become more dense, and as a result sink down into the asthenosphere again; each plate acts somewhat like a conveyor belt, in that new lithosphere is created on one side and old lithosphere destroyed on the other. The reason continents do not sink back into the asthenosphere is that their density is less than that of the asthenosphere. When a mass of light continental crust reaches the sinking edge of a plate, several things can happen—the most important thing, however, is that it is likely to slam into a piece of continent on the adjacent plate, and the collision will form a mountain range such as the Alps or the Himalaya. Although many details are still poorly understood, the distribution of certain classes of mineral deposits seem to be somehow related to the present and past edges that mark the bounds of moving plates; many scientists feel that a better understanding of plate movements, and of the mechanisms that cause the plates to move, will someday lead to a vastly improved understanding of how and why certain mineral deposits form.

The average composition of the continental crust (Fig. 2-4) reveals that only nine elements account for 99 percent of its total mass. The other 79 elements can thus only be present in minor and trace amounts. Many of the trace elements (or the minerals formed by one or more of the trace elements) turn out to be the very resources that are vital for modern day technology. Fortunately, there are a number of special ways in which local concentrations, or ores, of the scarcer elements have formed within the crust. Before discussing how these elements were concentrated, and how large the concentrations are, let us look briefly at the outer zones of the earth.

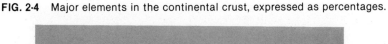

FIG. 2-4 Major elements in the continental crust, expressed as percentages.

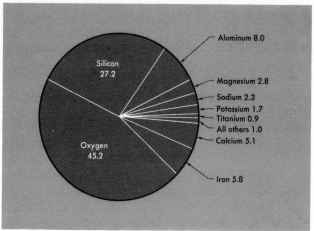

The Hydrosphere

The hydrosphere is the entire body of water, ice, and water vapor, on and near the surface of the earth. It is, to some extent, intermingled both with the atmosphere and with the crust; to an important degree, the crust and hydrosphere react with each other to cause such phenomena as weathering, the saltiness of the sea, and the compositions of the river and well water we drink.

Water itself is the most valuable resource of the hydrosphere, but there are many other important resources there. The oceans, which cover 70.8 percent of the earth's surface to an average depth of 3.96 kilometers, act as a collection reservoir for many of the soluble materials formed on the earth, such as those released from rocks and soils by weathering and those present in volcanic gases. The oceans have probably been salty throughout the ages, though it is possible that the degree of saltiness has changed. The present salinity is 3.5 percent dissolved solids by weight in solution. A salinity of 3.5 percent amounts to approximately 36×10^6 metric tons of dissolved matter in every cubic kilometer of seawater; the relative proportions of the major elements in solution are essentially constant throughout the world's oceans. Sodium and chlorine, the two elements present in common salt, are by far the most abundant dissolved elements; these, together with magnesium, sulfur, calcium, and potassium, account for 99.5 percent of all dissolved solids in the sea (Fig. 2-5). Each cubic kilometer of seawater contains significant amounts of 64 other elements; with small variations, each cubic kilometer contains, on the average, 2,000 kilograms each of zinc and copper; 800 kilograms of tin, 280 kilograms of silver, and 11 kilograms of gold.

Despite the fact that all chemical elements known in rocks are also

FIG. 2-5 Average composition of dissolved salts in seawater on a weight percentage basis.

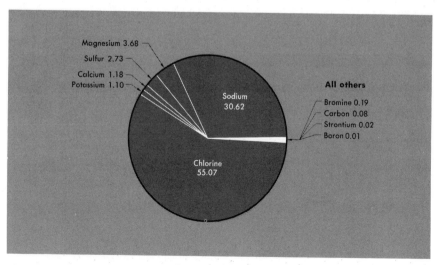

present in seawater, only four elements have been commercially recovered from seawater in significant quantities: sodium and chlorine (recovered jointly in the form of common salt), magnesium, and bromine. Sodium chloride is locally produced by solar evaporation of seawater in shallow ponds at many places around the world. Bromine is recovered by the addition of the complex organic compound aniline, which causes the precipitation of the nearby insoluble compound tribromoaniline, or by the addition of chlorine gas, which causes bromine gas to be released. (The starting solution for this process is usually seawater from which sodium chloride has already been removed.) Magnesium is recovered by the addition of dissolved calcium hydroxide to seawater, or to the residue of seawater from which other salts have been removed by evaporation; magnesium hydroxide is precipitated in the process.

The composition of seawater is well established, and the volume of the ocean basins has been measured accurately. The marine resources of the few elements that we are now recovering commercially must therefore be classified as reserves. These reserves are enormous and seem capable of filling every conceivable future demand. The potential resources of the other elements, including those that are present in trace amounts but that are not presently recovered, are also known with a high degree of certainty. Because the volume of the seas is $1,375 \times 10^6$ cubic kilometers, the potential resources are truly enormous, and one must ask why they are not exploited more extensively. There are two obvious difficulties. Unless specific reactions can be found to remove only the element or elements of interest, as in the removal of bromine by precipitation of tribromoaniline, all the other dissolved compounds must also be removed—a process that is expensive because it consumes a vast amount of energy and is wasteful unless uses can be found for the large amounts of materials so produced. Furthermore, although the total amounts of minor elements present in the sea are large, the solution is still an exceedingly dilute one, for most elements, and enormous amounts of water must be processed in order to recover the small quantities dissolved.

It is interesting to compare the average composition of rocks of the continental crust with that of seawater. Valuable elements such as gold and copper are much more abundant in crustal rocks (Table 2-1). If we ever do reach the day when identifiable mineral deposits can no longer supply our needs for metals, and we must rely either on average rocks or seawater, the numbers in Table 2-1 suggest that the odds are strongly in favor of common rocks. The odds could, of course, be tipped in favor of seawater if an extraction process were found that would be at least a thousand times more efficient than a comparable extraction process from rocks. Unfortunately, the extreme dilution of most elements in seawater makes this difficult because of the sheer volume of water that must be handled. It has been estimated, for example, that if seawater must be pumped during processing, and if a plant capable of handling a volume as great as 4.5 million liters a minute works with a 100 percent extraction efficiency, the cost of pumping and processing would exceed the

Table 2-1 Contents of Some Important Elements in a Cubic Kilometer of Average Continental Crust and of Average Seawater

Metal	Amount in Continental Crust (metric tons)	Amount in Seawater (metric tons)
SODIUM	69,000,000	11,020,000
POTASSIUM	51,000,000	396,000
CHLORINE	5,700,000	19,800,000
MANGANESE	1,809,000	1.9
ZINC	170,000	2
CHROMIUM	130,000	0.2
BROMINE	120,000	68,000
NICKEL	100,000	2
COPPER	86,000	2
COBALT	32,000	0.05
URANIUM	7,800	3.3
TIN	5,700	0.8
SILVER	160	0.3
GOLD	5	0.01

present value of the extracted material for all elements less abundant than boron. If pumping could be avoided, costs would clearly be much lower. One possible pump-free extraction process has already been tested. Seawater contains approximately 3.3 metric tons of uranium per cubic kilometer. This can be extracted when seawater is passed over titanium hydroxide coated on glass fibers. An intriguing suggestion, made some years ago, was that pumping could be avoided if bags of such fibers could be exposed to tidal currents or used as linings on the bottoms of ships. The process was proved in the laboratory and then tested using tidal currents in the Irish Sea. The large-scale test is reported to have been highly uneconomic. Similarly innovative new chemical extraction methods that are economically attractive may some day be found for other elements; the rewards, like the problems, could be enormous. Unfortunately, most authorities view the chances of success as remote. We must conclude, therefore, that for sodium, potassium, magnesium, calcium, and strontium; for the halogen elements chlorine, bromine, iodine, and fluorine; and for sulfur, boron, and phosphorus, the sea contains vast potential resources that might some day be exploited. The sea also contains vast amounts of a large number of other elements, but these are unlikely ever to be exploited because there are more favorable sources of the same elements in crustal rocks.

The limited possibilities for commercially extracting elements from seawater should not divert our attention from the possibility that there are mineral resources in rocks on the floor of the ocean (manganese nodules, and the recently discovered copper-zinc deposits along the East Pacific Rise, for example), or that there are possible energy sources in seawater. These possibilities are discussed later in the book.

The Atmosphere

The atmosphere is continually mixed and has an essentially uniform composition; it is also accessible and easy to sample. The composition of the atmosphere is relatively simple and is known with great accuracy; estimates of the abundance of the few atmospheric gases we use fall into the category of reserves. Three gases—nitrogen, oxygen, and argon—account for 99.9 percent of the atmospheric volume; nitrogen, an essential element in plant fertilizers, is the most abundant constituent.

Oxygen and argon, together with the rarer gases, neon, xenon, and krypton, are also recovered from the atmosphere, but in relatively small amounts. The uses to which these gases are put do not permanently remove them from the atmosphere; thus, we can classify them as renewable resources. The amounts used are so small that their temporary removal has no observable effect on the composition of the atmosphere.

For the few recoverable elements concentrated in it, the atmosphere provides an essentially limitless source.

GEOCHEMICAL CYCLING

We are aware of the facts that the earth is a dynamic body and that movement is continual. Winds are always blowing in the atmosphere, the sea is continually stirred by currents and waves, rain and snow fall from the skies, and the water runs down to the sea through myriad channels. By now it will also be apparent that the solid earth is a dynamic body too. Continents slide around on larger plates of lithosphere; collisions occur and mountains are thrust up; weathering and erosion slowly erode mountains away; the sediment is transported to the oceans by streams, and eventually new sedimentary rocks are formed. The processes are all repeated again and again, one cycle of events after another.

All of earth's zones are influenced and controlled by cycles. Weathering of rocks and transportation of sediment, for example, involve the crust, atmosphere, and hydrosphere. Water from the hydrosphere and gases from the atmosphere penetrate and react with rocks of the crust to cause weathering. In the process the composition of each zone is changed in some small way. Water from the hydrosphere and gases from the atmosphere, such as carbon dioxide and oxygen, are consumed in some of the chemical reactions that occur during weathering. But there are also reactions that release gases and water—reactions such as photosynthesis by plants, which adds oxygen to the atmosphere, and metamorphism of sedimentary rocks, which releases carbon dioxide and water. As a result of the multitude of cycles involving interactions between the mantle, crust, biosphere, atmosphere, and hydrosphere, each zone has developed and maintains a distinctive composition. We refer to the cycling of materials as *geochemical cycles,* and to the stable compositions that result as the *geochemical balance.*

All of the mineral deposits found in the crust have been formed as a result of one or more geochemical cycles. There are many important conclusions that can be drawn from a study of the cycles. Two conclusions deserve special mention. The first concerns the energy that drives the cycles: The energy comes both from earth's internal heat—for it is that which causes plates of lithosphere to move, continents to collide, and volcanoes to form—and from the sun's heat, which warms the surface and thereby causes winds, waves, currents, rain, erosion, and most of the other phenomena at earth's surface. A planet that is devoid of internal heat and volcanic activity and that does not have a hydrosphere would not have the geochemical cycles that form most kinds of mineral deposits. Earth's complement of mineral deposits is unique to earth and reflects the kinds and intensity of cycles that operate here.

The second important conclusion concerns the ever-increasing magnitude of human interference in geochemical cycles. We now form and build on so much of the land surface that we have altered the pattern of sediment transport around the world. We burn oil, natural gas, and coal in such vast quantities that the carbon dioxide released by the burning is slowly changing the composition of the atmosphere. There are many other obvious changes, such as those of polluted streams and harbors, acid rain, and contaminated wells. We are forced to conclude that human beings are probably influencing many geochemical cycles, some in small ways, some in large ways, and that if the changes continue, we may cause irreversible changes to earth's zones. It is ironic that exploitation of the mineral wealth concentrated through geological ages by geochemical cycles should now be the medium through which human beings are inadvertently causing disruption of the cycles.

energy from fossil fuels

When consideration is given to the factual data pertaining to both the world and the U.S. rates of production of coal and oil. . two results of outstanding significance become obvious. The first of these is the extreme brevity of the time during which most of these developments have occurred. For example, although coal has been mined for about 800 years, one-half of the coal produced during the period has been mined during the last 31 years. Half of the world's cumulative production of petroleum has occurred during the 12-year period since 1956.

The second obvious conclusion . . . is that the steady rates of growth sustained during a period of several decades . . . cannot be maintained for much longer periods of time. (M. King Hubbert, "Energy Resources," in Resources and Man, *edited by P. Cloud, 1969, U.S. National Academy of Sciences.)*

World energy consumption rose by about 30 percent between 1970 and 1978.

(The World Environment, 1972–1982. A Report by the United Nations Environment Programme. Vol. 8 in the Natural Resources and The Environment Series.)

We saw in Chapter 1 that energy resources are our most valuable mineral commodities. They are, therefore, the first resources to gain our attention.

Units and Sources of Energy

Before proceeding, let us clarify some terms. *Energy* is the capacity to do work. Units of measurement reflect the kind of work being done. For example, the *calorie* is defined as the heat needed to raise the temperature of 1 gram of water by 1°C; the *joule* is the energy needed to maintain an electrical current of 1 ampere for 1 second at a potential of 1 volt. Energy can, of course, be converted from one form to another; energy units, therefore, are interchangeable. 1 joule is equal to 0.239 calories. There are many energy units in common use in addition to the joule and the calorie; examples are the British thermal unit (Btu) and the erg. To avoid the confusion that arises when changing from one system to another, we will use only the joule.

Although the total available energy is an important number, we must also be concerned with the *rate* at which energy is used, and this means that a time-dependent property must be introduced. This property is called *power* and is a measure of energy produced or used in a fixed unit of time. The most familiar power unit is probably the horsepower, an old unit adopted in 1766 by James Watt in order to compare the working rate of horses with that of steam engines. The power unit used in this book is the *watt,* named for the same James Watt and defined as 1 joule per second. The watt, equivalent to 1.341×10^{-3} horsepower, is an especially important unit in discussions of renewable resources. For purposes of current energy consumption, for example, the total amount of solar energy that has reached the earth in the past, and the amount that will reach it in the future, are not important; the important figure is the rate at which it arrives presently, because that is the maximum rate at which it can be used.

Man's Use of Energy

The amount of energy now used by mankind to supplement human muscle energy is enormous. In 1983, the people of the world used an estimated 2.6×10^{20} joules of supplementary energy drawn from sources such as coal, oil, natural gas, and hydroelectric and nuclear power plants. We cannot know exactly how much wood and animal dung are burned every day in the millions of cooking fires in the many countries of Asia and Africa, but the amount must be quite large; when added to the figure of 2.6×10^{20} joules, it must raise the total supplementary energy used by all the peoples of the world to at least 3.0×10^{20} joules. This is an average power consumption of 9.5×10^{12} watts. Considering just the certain figure of 2.6×10^{20} joules, in 1983, the per capita consumption of energy by the world's 4.4 billion people was 60×10^{9} joules, equivalent to the burning of 2 metric tons of coal or about 10 barrels of oil for every living man, woman, and child. The per capita consumption on a worldwide scale is growing steadily, even though in some industrial countries the rate of growth has declined (Fig. 3-1).

Nevertheless, this amount is still tiny by comparison with the solar energy that reaches the earth *each day:* 1.5×10^{22} joules. Clearly, the problem with energy as a resource is not the total amount available, but rather the amounts available from the sources we prefer and are able to use. At present only a small fraction of our supplementary energy comes from renewable sources—hydroelectric schemes, solar heating, wood burning, wind and water wheels. By far the greatest amount comes from nonrenewable sources, particularly from the fossil fuels, coal, oil, and natural gas (Fig. 3-2). From Fig. 3-2, we can see that the world's dependence on oil and natural gas is continuing to increase at the expense of coal and hydroelectricity. The situation in an industrial country such as the United States differs but little from that of the

FIG. 3-1 Per capita consumptions of supplementary energy other than from sources such as wood and dung used for cooking fires. Inhabitants of industrial countries such as Japan, England, and the United States have much higher consumption rates than do inhabitants of developing countries that are primarily agrarian, such as Burma and Tanzania. (Data from United Nations.)

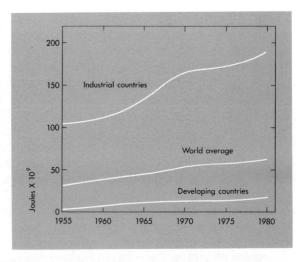

world as a whole. On a global basis, natural gas supplies 21 percent and crude oil 45 percent of the supplementary energy. In the United States, the extensive net of gas pipelines makes use of gas rather easy; thus, the figure for natural gas is 37 percent and for crude oil 32 percent.

In any discussion of natural resources, the manner in which resources are used is particularly important. This is especially true where energy resources are concerned, because the way energy is made available largely determines the way it is used. For example, nuclear power stations produce electricity, but electricity does not help the truck driver who needs gasoline.

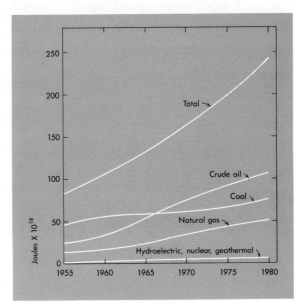

FIG. 3-2 Supplementary energy used in the world is drawn from many sources, but principally from coal, crude oil, and natural gas. (Data from United Nations.)

The use of energy in an industrial community such as the United States (Fig. 3-3), therefore, raises many interesting points. There is an inherent loss whenever energy is stored, transported, or converted from one form to another. This limitation is set by the laws of nature. A significant fraction of the lost energy, however, is due to our own inefficiency and waste.

FOSSIL FUELS

The term *fossil fuel* refers to organic remains of plants and animals trapped in sedimentary rock. Fossil fuels occur in many ways, depending on the kind of sediment, the nature of the original organic compounds, and the changes that have occurred through long geological ages.

Living organisms derive their energy from the sun. The principal energy-trapping mechanism is photosynthesis, the process by which plants use the sun's energy to combine water and carbon dioxide to make carbohydrates plus the oxygen we breathe from the atmosphere. When animals eat plants, organic compounds are the fuels that keep them alive and active; animals are therefore secondary consumers of trapped solar energy. When plants are eaten or when they die and decay, the trapped energy is released and the organic matter is broken down again to water and carbon dioxide.

In many sediments, a little organic matter is trapped and buried before it is completely removed by decay. Thus, some of the solar energy becomes stored in rocks—hence the term *fossil fuel*. The rate of plant and animal decay is very nearly equal to the rate of photosynthesis, and the fraction of organic

FIG. 3-3 Flow and use of supplementary energy in the United States during 1982, expressed as a percentage of the total energy use. Some oil and gas are used for non-energy purposes, principally for production of petrochemicals. Although the percentages drawn from different energy sources change somewhat from year to year, the uses and efficiencies remain about the same. (After J.D. Morgan, U.S. Bureau of Mines.)

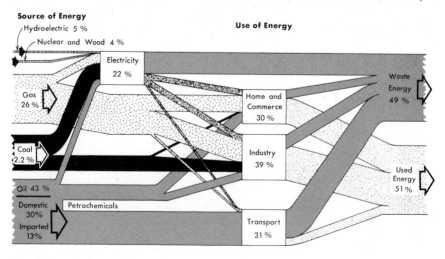

matter that becomes trapped is tiny. Nevertheless, the plant remains that have accumulated during the billion years or so that life has been prolifically distributed across the earth is now considerable. The accumulation rate has been millions of times slower than the rate at which we now dig up organic matter and burn it—we must therefore consider the fossil fuels to be nonrenewable resources. There is organic matter in virtually every sedimentary rock. Most, however, is sparse or difficult to extract; to date we have only learned to use three kinds of fossil fuels: coal, crude oil, and natural gas. The "big three" now supply over 95 percent of the world's supplementary energy (Fig. 3-2), but it is probable that other sources, such as solid organic matter in the fine-grain sediment and especially the variety called oil shale, will someday be used.

Coal

Coal forms from the remains of freshwater plants. Dead limbs, trunks, leaves, seeds, and spores fall into densely vegetated swamps where they become waterlogged and sink. Once covered by water and protected from the atmosphere, bacterial digestion turns the wood plant remains to a jellylike mass of peat. Oxygen supplies in stagnant water are quickly consumed, the bacteria die, decay ceases, and the peat accumulates. Thick deposits can form only if the swamp slowly subsides during accumulation, and rich deposits only occur when the inflow of mud and other debris (erroneously called ash) is slow. Sites of coal accumulation are not widespread on the earth at present; the Dismal Swamp of Virginia and North Carolina is a typical site; an average of 2 meters of modern peat there covers an area of 5,700 square kilometers.

The earliest fossils of land and freshwater plants occur in rocks about 410 million years old, suggesting that a transition from primitive to complex freshwater flora probably occurred about that time; before that time, the exposed lands of the world would only have supported mosses, lichens, and algae, and must have looked very different from the exposed lands of today's world. The oldest coal deposits occur in 370-million-year-old rocks; the most ancient coals of significant size are in the Canadian Arctic and are about 350 million years old. The greatest coal-forming period in the earth's history occurred between 350 and 250 million years ago. Coal deposits formed during this hundred-million-year time span have been found on all continents, but by far the greatest deposits were laid down in North America, Europe, and Asia. During the great Permian and Carboniferous coal-forming periods, North America, Europe, and Asia were, for long periods, in temperate and equatorial latitudes where warm climates and high rainfall favored the development of enormous swamps. The present-day Southern Hemisphere continents, South America, Australia, Africa, were only in warm climates for relatively short periods and by contrast spent long periods in high, cold latitudes. Subsequent periods of coal formation have occurred, especially the Cretaceous, but none has been as extensive or as prolific as the great coal age that ended 250 million years ago.

Peat, the first stage in the formation of coal, is a low-rank material, which is to say that it has a high water content and a relatively low carbon content and therefore a low heat-producing or calorific value. A series of reactions occur upon burial and compaction of peat. Much of the water, oxygen, nitrogen, and other compounds originally present in the plants are expelled, leaving an increasingly dense and carbon-rich coal. The process of coalification proceeds with age, bringing an increase in rank (Fig. 3-4), so that older and more deeply buried coals generally are of higher rank than younger or shallower ones. One fortunate consequence of the fact that the great coal-forming period ended 250 million years ago is that by far the largest amount of coal is today of high rank. The World Energy Conference of 1980 estimated that when all known coals and peats are compared on the basis of their calorific values, 62 percent are bituminous coals or anthracites, 28.3 percent are sub-bituminous coals, while only 8.6 percent are lignite, and 1.1 percent are peat.

A great many coal basins have been remarkably stable and have been subjected neither to metamorphism nor to rapid erosion since they formed. Some geologists believe that most of the coal ever formed is still on earth.

FIG. 3-4 Increasing calorific value of coal with increasing rank.

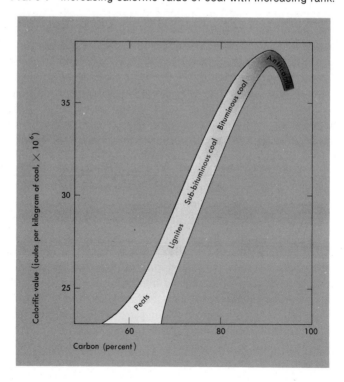

They also believe that most (but not necessarily all) of the major coal basins have already been discovered. On this basis, P. Averitt of the U.S. Geological Survey in 1969 published the most extensive analysis of the world's coal supplies to date. By making some specific assumptions regarding recoverability, Averitt estimated the world's reserves of all forms of coal to be 8,620 billion metric tons, and the additional potential resources to be 6,650 billion metric tons. Averitt considered coal to be recoverable if it occurred in seams greater than 30 centimeters thick and was no deeper than 2,000 meters. Coal that did not meet these requirements—for example, the extension of well-known seams below the cut-off mining depths—was said to be a potential resource. The magnitude of the potential resource is reasonably well known in the case of coal, so there is some justification for combining reserves and potential resources for a total of 15,270 billion metric tons, equivalent in heat energy to about 4.2×10^{23} joules. How much coal Averitt excluded by selecting 30 centimeters as a cutoff is not known, but the amount is probably not very large. Unfortunately, it seems to be impossible to mine all the coal from a seam, and in many cases of underground mining, a recovery of 50 percent is considered excellent. Using a conservative 50 percent as the figure for the recoverable fraction of the world's coal, Dr. Averitt estimated we may eventually recover 7,135 billion metric tons of coal, equivalent to about 2.1×10^{23} joules. As seen in Fig. 3-5, the geographic distribution of coal reserves is highly erratic. There have been a number of studies of coal reserves subsequent to Averitt's

FIG. 3-5 Geographic distribution of coal reserves. Most of the recoverable coal occurs in North America, Europe, and Asia, leaving the continents of the Southern Hemisphere relatively coal-poor.

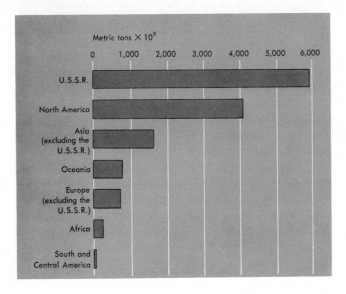

study, but they change his figures very little. The World Energy Conference of 1980, for example, raised the figure for estimated recoverable resources of all forms of coal to 13,800 billion metric tons. They added newly discovered coal in Australia, but they were also more liberal in their interpretation of what is recoverable than was Averitt. Regardless of exactly how much coal we accept as recoverable, the distribution patterns remain very similar: About 43 percent of the world's coal lies within the borders of the U.S.S.R., 29 percent in North America, 14.5 is in Asian countries outside of the U.S.S.R—mainly in China—and 5.5 percent in Europe. The rest of the world has only 8 percent.

The widespread use of coal as a fuel began in the twelfth century A.D., when inhabitants of the northeast coast of England found that inflammable black rocks weathering out of coastal cliffs were good substitutes for their rapidly disappearing forest woods. Known as "sea coles" because of the black color that resembled coal from a wood fire, the new fuel soon became widely used—to the extent that by 1273 outraged Londoners complained of repugnant odors and air pollution arising from coal burning. This deterred no one, however, and the use of coal as a fuel spread rapidly. Although coal is not the predominant source of energy in the world, it is still predominant in some countries, and the probable limitations on the supplies of oil and gas suggest that the use of coal might increase rapidly in the decades ahead. It is possible that by the year 2020 coal may once again be the world's predominant fossil fuel.

As desirable as coal might be for a fuel, many difficulties attend its use. Coal contains from 0.2 percent to about 7 percent sulfur, present mostly in the mineral pyrite, FeS_2; in ferrous sulfate, $FeSO_4 \cdot 7H_2O$; in gypsum, $CaSO_4 \cdot 2H_2O$; and in some of the organic compounds. When coal is burned, oxidized sulfur is released, and if this is allowed to reach the atmosphere it can cause serious environmental hazards such as smog and acid rain. Low-sulfur coal can be burned without serious consequences, but most coal has to be processed during or prior to burning in order to reduce the level of sulfur emissions. Treatment costs are high, and concerns have been expressed by many experts concerning the reliability of extraction. The acrid, sulfurous odors that annoyed Londoners in 1273 are proof that the problem is a long-standing one. Another problem of vital concern is the mining of coal. Extraction by underground methods is unpleasant and inherently dangerous; it seems to carry the long-term threat of unavoidable health hazards. Surface mining is more efficient and less dangerous than underground mining but causes serious disruption of the land surface. Furthermore, only about 4 percent of all coal lies close enough to the surface or occurs in thick enough seams to be recovered by strip mining. For the United States this amounts to some 130 billion metric tons out of a total of 3,900 billion metric tons. In the long run, therefore, underground extraction of coal, despite its many difficulties, will presumably be the predominant recovery method.

Crude Oil and Natural Gas

All of the organic matter trapped in sediments is originally solid. A small fraction of the solid matter can, with a suitable rise in temperature, undergo a series of chemical changes during which a portion is converted to liquids and gases. These liquids and gases are the precursors of crude oil and natural gas, jointly called petroleum. The much larger quantity of remaining solid organic matter can, if subjected to still higher temperatures and pressures, be further converted to liquids and gases, but an unconverted residue always remains. It is solid organic matter in fine-grained sedimentary rocks that have not been heated to high temperatures that engineers propose to recover and process, in the so-called oil shales, by providing the necessary temperature and pressure to effect conversion to petroleum liquids and gases.

Crude oil and natural gas are composed chiefly of a family of chemical compounds called *hydrocarbons* and, like coal, are found in sedimentary rocks (Fig. 3-6). Although not confined to marine sedimentary rocks, petroleum is more abundant there than in freshwater rocks, and it is conspicuously more abundant in sedimentary basins with a high percentage of fine-grained, organic-rich sediments. All sediments contain some organic debris and a wide variety of petroleum hydrocarbons, and even tiny droplets of crude oil can be found associated with solid organic matter in many common rocks such as shales and limestones. There is little doubt, therefore, that widespread sedimentary organic matter, of microscopic plant and animal origin, must be the source of petroleum; further, it would seem that petroleum formation begins immediately after burial of the organic matter.

The earliest formed petroleum compounds tend to have high molecular weights, like those in the solid matter from which they are derived, and produce very viscous oils. On burial, and as the temperature and pressure rise, the large molecules are continually broken or *cracked* into lighter and more mobile ones. The longer the process continues, the "lighter," or less viscous, the crude oil becomes. Although the elemental chemical composition does not change much, and most crude oils and natural gases fall in a small bulk chemical composition range (Table 3-1), the diversity of individual compounds produced is so great that no two oils ever contain exactly the same molecular mix.

As the hydrocarbon molecules become lighter and more mobile, they migrate readily. The exact details of migration in any given sedimentary basin remain uncertain, but it is clear that as sediment piles deepen, the oil, gas, and water that fill the pores between the mineral grains are slowly squeezed out and migrate toward the surface. The fine-grained, organic-rich shale layers that are sources for most of the oil and gas tend to be almost impermeable, because the connecting passages between individual pores are tiny, and fluids move through them very slowly. The first step in the migration process, therefore, is slow movement by the oil and gas to adjacent, more permeable sed-

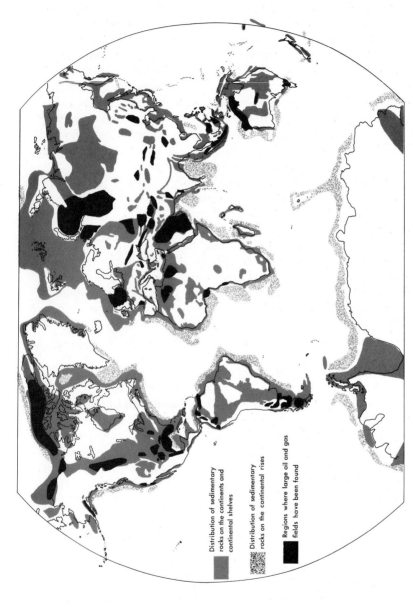

FIG. 3-6 Sedimentary rocks and regions where oil and gas have been located. The continental shelf and slope, extending out to a water depth of 2,000 meters, contain large potential resources of petroleum, particularly where they are underlain by seaward projec- tions of sedimentary basins. Thick piles of young sediments beyond the continental slope, a region sometimes called the continental rise, are also believed to contain large petroleum resources.

Distribution of sedimentary rocks on the continents and continental shelves

Distribution of sedimentary rocks on the continental rises

Regions where large oil and gas fields have been found

Table 3-1 Composition of Typical Petroleum

Element	Crude Oil (percent)	Natural Gas (percent)
CARBON	82.2–87.0	65–80
HYDROGEN	11.7–14.7	1–25
SULFUR	0.1– 5.5	trace–0.2
NITROGEN	0.1– 1.5	1–15
OXYGEN	0.1– 4.5	—

(From Geology of Petroleum, Second Edition, by A.I. Levorsen. W.H. Freeman and Company, Copyright 1967.)

imentary layers such as sandstones and limestones. Within permeable layers fluids flow laterally through the connecting pore spaces due to the pressure of the overlying rocks. Oil and gas are lighter than water and tend to become concentrated in the upper part of a permeable layer. If there are barriers or traps along the migration paths, the oil and gas will accumulate, filling most of the pores in the trap (Fig. 3-7). It is important to realize that a so-called oil or gas "pool" is in fact solid rock and that only the pore spaces contain oil and gas. The success with which the oil and gas can be recovered depends in large part on how rapidly the oil and gas will flow out of the pores and into the wells we drill.

The fact that oil and gas escape slowly from a pile of sedimentary rocks is substantiated by the observation that the highest ratios of oil pools to volume of sediments tend to be found in the youngest group of oil-bearing sed-

FIG. 3-7 Types of oil traps and reservoir rocks, together with the percentage of the world's oil production from each. (From *Man's Physical World* by J.E. Van Riper. Copyright 1962 by McGraw-Hill, Inc. Used with permission of McGraw-Hill Book Company.)

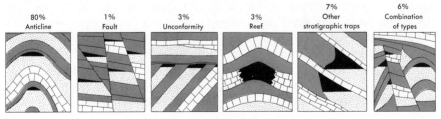

80% Anticline	1% Fault	3% Unconformity	3% Reef	7% Other stratigraphic traps	6% Combination of types

Types of oil traps

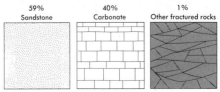

59% Sandstone	40% Carbonate	1% Other fractured rocks

Type of reservoir rock

iments, deposited no later than 2.5 million years ago. It is also substantiated by the observation that the total amount of trapped oil and gas tends to decrease the further we move back in time. Indeed, until very recently it was believed there were no substantial oil or gas accumulations older than the Cambrian, 570 million years, even though organic-rich shales more than twice that age have long been known. Now it has been demonstrated in the U.S.S.R. and to a lesser extent in Australia that considerably older Proterozoic sediments may also contain gas fields, although the ratio of trapped gas to sediment volume is apparently quite low.

Natural gas, which is the lightest hydrocarbon fraction, and in particular methane, CH_4, may range from a small quantity dissolved in the crude oil, through a gaseous capping over an oil pool, to a separate accumulation not associated with a nearby oil pool. All such accumulations are valuable, and the technological mastery of pipeline-laying and more recently of commercial liquefaction has made natural gas widely available as fuel.

Petroleum, like coal, is widespread but unevenly distributed. The reasons for such a distribution are not as obvious as they are with coal. The kinds of organic-rich sediment that can be sources for petroleum are very widespread, but they must be subjected to reasonably high temperatures in order to convert enough of the solid organic matter to oil and gas, and the conversion must occur while some of the sediments are still permeable and can act as conduits for the migrating fluids. Even if all other conditions are favorable, the actual trapping of oil is a matter of delicate timing. Most oil and gas fields are found in traps that formed by flexing and fracturing of the host rocks. The traps must, of course, form before most of the oil and gas migrate away and escape, and this seems to be a rather haphazard business. Almost all sedimentary rocks are deformed at some time in their history, because earth's seemingly solid surface is actually rather mobile and is continually subjected to slow vertical and lateral movements. Most deformation apparently takes place after the main period of petroleum formation and migration, so most of the oil and gas that is formed is never trapped and just slowly leaks away. Geologists estimate that the chance of petroleum formation coinciding with formation of suitable large traps is so low that no more than 0.1 percent of the organic matter deposited in oil-source rocks is eventually trapped in oil pools. Where all factors coincide, however, as in Saudi Arabia, Kuwait, and Iraq, truly enormous amounts of petroleum can be trapped. As many as 50 billion barrels of oil may eventually be recovered from the largest Saudi oil fields discovered to date.

Production and consumption of petroleum have reached such tremendous proportions that it is sobering to remember that the first natural gas well was drilled in Fredonia, New York in 1821, and that commercial production of oil only began in 1857—little more than 100 years ago—in Rumania; this was followed 2 years later by production in the United States. World consumption of both crude oil and natural gas rose for many years at a rate of approximately 8.5 percent a year, which corresponds to a doubling period of 8 years. There was a brief worldwide decline in the rate at which oil was used following the oil crisis of 1973, but the steady upward rise has resumed since 1975 (Fig. 3-8). So vast is the use of oil and gas that the question of supply adequacy has become vital.

Although the oil and gas industries maintain adequate reserves for near-term production, they lack a reliable way of estimating the potential resources still to be discovered. Oil and gas pools are small compared with coal fields and can be located only at high cost and with considerable difficulty. However, we know where sedimentary rocks are to be found in the world (see Fig. 3-6), and if we assume that the oil potential in unexplored areas is just as good as it is in the most highly explored areas, it is possible to make a geological estimate of the world's ultimate recoverable resources of oil and gas. Various authorities have done this and have come up with answers that differ by factors of three or four. Part of the uncertainty lies in the percentage of oil accepted as recoverable from an already located field. The present figure of 35

FIG. 3-8 World production of crude oil. The temporary interruption in the steady upward rise came about as a result of the OPEC oil crisis of 1973. A conversion of 6 × 10⁹ joules per barrel was used. (Data from U.S. Bureau of Mines and United Nations.)

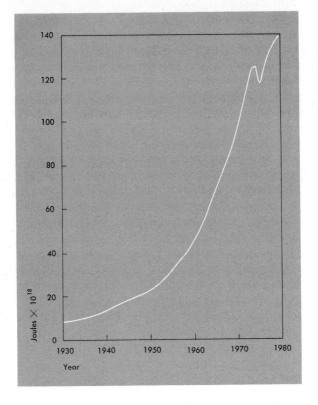

percent recovery, for example, is considered too low by some, realistic by others. Another source of uncertainty lies in one's evaluation of just how well explored the sedimentary basins of a developed area like the United States actually are. Combining oil and gas (by taking 1,470 cubic meters of gas as equal in heating capacity to 1 barrel of crude oil, or 6×10^9 joules), most estimates for the world's recoverable potential resources of petroleum lie in the range of 1×10^{22} joules to 2.6×10^{22} joules. These extremes include the oil and gas that remain to be found and developed on the continental shelf, on the continental slope, and in the great pile of sediments that have accumulated along the base of many continental slopes.

One of the most authoritative and also the most optimistic estimates for recoverable oil and gas was reported by the World Energy Conference of 1980. Converted to heating equivalents, the Conference figures for recoverable oil are 1.5×10^{22} joules, and for gas, 1.1×10^{22} joules. Figure 3-9 demonstrates how resources are distributed, how much is proven, and how much is already produced. Observe that the ratio of oil to gas varies from place to place. Some areas, such as North America, or the U.S.S.R. plus China and Eastern Europe, seem to be relatively gas rich, while Africa and the Middle East are relatively oil rich. Observe also the relatively high cumulative productions in North and South America.

How reliable are estimates of potential resources such as the ones given in Fig. 3-9? Until all the oil and gas have actually been produced, we can never be certain what the final figures will be. However, there is an independent observation that suggests that the figures might be reasonably reliable. In extensively explored and developed petroleum regions, geologists have observed that more than half of the total oil and gas occurs in a few giant fields. They also observe that the giant fields are the first to be found. The greatest uncertainty concerning the estimates in Fig. 3-9 should therefore be placed on the least explored areas—Antarctica, for which present estimates are so small that it is not even given a separate entry in Fig. 3-9, Australia, and China. Of course, the deep-water piles of sediments at the foot of the world's continental slopes also remain to be tested, and these too might be richer than is presently anticipated.

Many important conclusions can be drawn from Fig. 3-9 and from our present knowledge of oil and gas resources, but three deserve special mention. First, it is apparent that the regions that are now major oil or gas producers and that have the largest proven reserves also have the greatest future potential for new discoveries. The second conclusion to be drawn from Fig. 3-9 is that oil and gas resources are like many other mineral resources in that they are very unequally distributed around the world. As in the case of coal, the countries of the Southern Hemisphere seem to have the smaller share. The third conclusion comes from the estimated size of the oil and gas resource and the world's annual consumption rate, which passed 1.8×10^{20} joules in 1983. Even if, on a worldwide basis, the recoverable oil and gas resource amounts to an optimistic 2.6×10^{22} joules, the present growth rate would, if main-

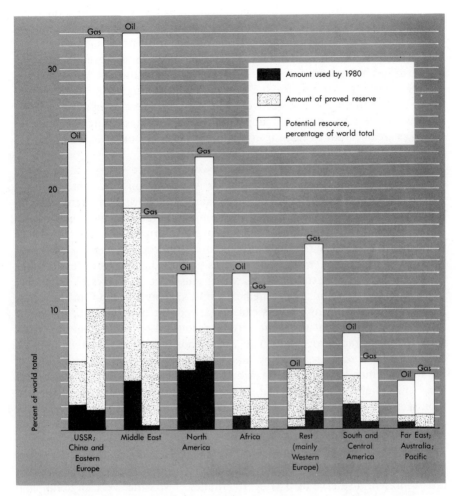

FIG. 3-9 Potential resources of oil and gas as a percentage of world total. Cumulative production and proven reserve for each region to 1980. The energy equivalent of the estimated potential resources of oil is 1.5×10^{22} joules and of gas is 1.1×10^{22} joules. (After World Energy Conference, 1980.)

tained, consume half the total by the year 2003 and, presuming that gas replaces oil as oil resources are depleted, the entire amount by the year 2015. This situation will not be so drastic because other fuels will be increasingly used long before this date, but the example demonstrates that the history of oil and gas may be a short one—little more than 150 years.

Tar Sand, Shale Oil, and Other Fossil Fuels

When crude oil is pumped from a well drilled into an oil pool, as much as 60 percent of the oil originally in the pool remains trapped in pore spaces between mineral grains, as coatings on minerals, and in the innumerable tiny holes and fractures of rocks. Over geologically long times the trapped oil might trickle slowly into the well, but for the practical purpose of producing oil today, this is no help. The trapped fraction of an oil pool is, in effect, not recoverable by present methods. Some success has been achieved in speeding up flow rates by such means as blasting and fracturing the reservoir rocks, by heating the ground, and by forcing high pressure carbon dioxide or steam into the reservoir, but secondary recovery methods still leave as much as half of the original oil in the ground. Trapped oil thus constitutes a potential resource that is as great as that of flowing crude oil, but it is a resource that will require very innovative technology if it is ever to be used.

Oil that is particularly thick and viscous is called heavy oil, or, more colloquially, bitumen, tar, or asphalt. Tar is a crude oil that contains large-molecule hydrocarbons, but it does not readily run, flow, or migrate, remaining in place as a cementing agent for the mineral grains of the porous sandstone. For the hydrocarbons to be recovered, processes similar to those employed in secondary recovery must be used; the rock itself must be heated with steam or flushed with a gas such as carbon dioxide in order to make the tar flow, and the resulting tarry extract must then be processed to recover the valuable oil fraction. For some heavy oils, such as those in California, the heating and gas-flushing process can be carried out underground, but many tars are so viscous that they can only be recovered by mining the reservoir, followed by surface processing. Thus, for deposits to be useful, they must be shallow enough to be reached by mining. Fortunately, the largest deposit in the world, which lies in northern Alberta and is known as the Athabasca Tar Sand (Fig. 3-10), can be reached by mining. These sands are now being exploited in a small way near Fort McMurray. However, technical problems are proving very difficult and costly, and widespread recovery of tars will possibly not occur until the next century.

The Athabasca Tar Sands cover an area of at least 75,000 square kilometers, reach thicknesses of 60 meters, and, if we assume a 50 percent recovery rate, represent a reserve of 0.31×10^{22} joules. Two other very large tar sand deposits are known. The Orinoco deposit in Venezuala is estimated to be almost as large as the Canadian deposit, but it is deeper and will be more difficult to recover. The Olenek deposit in the U.S.S.R. is reported to be about the same size as the Athabasca Sands, but again it suffers from recovery problems. No other large deposits are yet known in the world, but many small ones have been located during the search for crude oil. If we make the assumption that direct exploration for heavy oil will turn up some presently unknown large deposits, and that at least 50 percent can eventually be recovered, many authorities suggest that the heavy oil potential is about equal to the potential crude oil plus natural gas, namely 2.5×10^{22} joules.

Just as tars and heavy oils promise a continued production future for petroleum, so are there unconventional sources of natural gas that may someday be produced. Natural gas—principally methane, CH_4—is a common prod-

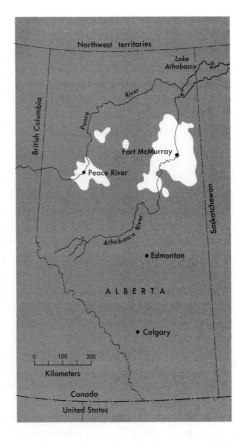

FIG. 3-10 Areas in Alberta, Canada, known to be underlain by tar sands. The first commercial production began near Fort McMurray, but extensive development of the resource may possibly not occur until the twenty-first century.

uct from degradation of organic matter. As a result, natural gas is present in many sedimentary rock units that are very tight, meaning that they have low permeability. But recovering gas from tight formations is expensive and technologically difficult, because the host rock must somehow be broken to increase permeability. Additionally, the pores in many sedimentary strata are filled with brines that are under pressure much greater than the hydrostatic pressure. The high pressures allow methane to dissolve in the brines, and the result is a huge potential natural gas resource in what is commonly referred to as *geopressured aquifers*. The best known geopressured region is in the United States, along the Texas-Louisiana coast, where there is a region that is up to 100 kilometers wide and many hundreds of kilometers long. Here, sedimentary rocks as deep as 16,000 meters contain geopressured aquifers filled with a solution of methane in hot brine.

How much of the gas in tight sands and shales or in geopressured aquifers can eventually be recovered remains an open question. One report, published in 1980, estimated that gas from unconventional sources, equivalent to 0.07×10^{22} joules, could already be produced around the world, but this amount is tiny by comparison with the 4.5×10^{22} joules estimated by the U.S. Government to lie within the geopressured aquifers of the United States alone. The potential resources of unconventional natural gas are clearly huge, possibly as large as 10×10^{22} joules, but the recoverable fraction remains very uncertain and is another example of an opportunity for technical advances.

A final kind of fossil organic matter is an even larger resource than coal, but unfortunately much of it is unlikely to ever be recovered. All sedimentary rock contains some organic matter, and the common fine-grained variety, shale, often contains enough so that petroleum can be extracted by heating the rock in order to effect the necessary chemical conversions. It is estimated that if organic matter in all the shales of the world were recovered and used for fuel, the resource would provide at least 10^{26} joules of energy and possibly more. But there is a severe catch to this apparently optimistic figure.

Processing the shale uses energy for mining and heating. It can readily be calculated that energy equivalent to burning 40 liters of oil would be used in processing a metric ton of shale. Most shales won't yield 40 liters of oil or the equivalent in gas, however, so unless some new and innovative way can be found to recover the oil, ordinary shale cannot be considered a potential energy resource. Only shales richer than 40 liters to the metric ton can be considered. The richest deposits known, in Estonia, yield up to 320 liters to the metric ton.

The United States is fortunate in possessing the world's largest known reserve of rich oil shale. During the Eocene epoch, three large shallow lakes existed in the intermontane area of Colorado, Wyoming, and Utah; in them was deposited the series of rich organic materials that are now oil shales (Fig. 3-11). Commonly known as the Green River Oil Shales, they are capable, in places, of producing up to 240 liters of oil per metric ton. Reserve estimates by the U.S. Geological Survey are enormous. Considering only shales capable of yielding 40 liters or more per metric ton, and assuming that half of the shales can be mined and processed, the Green River Shales are a potential resource of 0.75×10^{22} joules. Most of this potential is in the Piceance Basin of Colorado.

Production of oil from shale has been successfully carried out in Estonia, in the U.S.S.R., and in China for many years. Though scattered attempts at commercial production of the huge Green River Shales have been made, and technical feasibility has been demonstrated, none has yet proven commercially competitive with oil and natural gas. Commercial exploitation in the Piceance Basin has been considered by several large companies, and many people are concerned about the possible side effects. Mining would have to occur on a vast scale. Furthermore, distillation of the shale would produce a fine, sooty residue that would be puffed up and therefore larger in volume than the original shale. Disposal of this unpleasant residue is viewed as a major problem.

The United States contains many other oil shale resources in addition to the Green River Shales, but none is as rich or as readily treated. The U.S. Geological Survey estimates that with a yield of 40 liters from sediments at

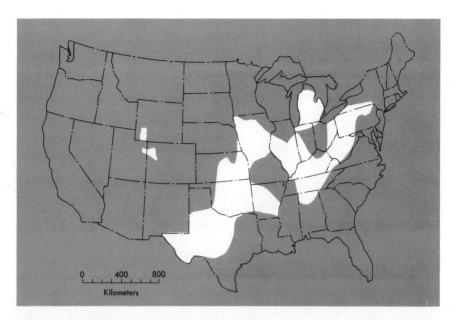

FIG. 3-11 A large part of the United States is underlain by organic-rich shales close enough to the surface to be mined and capable of yielding 40 liters or more of oil per metric ton. The richest oil shales are found in Colorado, Utah, and Wyoming. (After U.S. Geological Survey, 1969.)

least 1.5 meters thick and a mining efficiency of only 50 percent, the United States' potential resource might be as large as 7×10^{22} joules. Much of this potential lies in the central and eastern part of the country (Fig. 3-11). To mine such a huge area seems unthinkable, and once again we seem to be seeking new and innovative technology.

Rich oil shale resources in other parts of the world have not been adequately explored, but other huge deposits, such as those in Queensland, Australia, have already been found. The Irati Shales in southeast Brazil, perhaps half as large as the Green River Oil Shales in the United States, are the biggest units known outside North America. Lower grade resources, however, are just as abundant on other continents as they are in the United States. Accurate assessments have not been made, but if the 40 liter yield and 50 percent recovery figures are used, informed estimates by U.S. Geological Survey scientists indicate a worldwide potential resource of 10^{24} joules.

COMPARISON OF FOSSIL FUEL RESOURCES

Although the resource numbers derived for the fossil fuels all seem very large (Table 3-2), this must not lead us to a feeling of complacency. First, we should not overlook the fact that most of the large numbers are for potential resources that are either still to be found or for materials we still have to learn

Table 3-2 Potential Resources of Fossil Fuels*

Fuel	Amount in the Ground (joules $\times 10^{22}$)	Amount Possibly Recoverable (joules $\times 10^{22}$)
COAL	42	21
OIL AND GAS (flowing)	2.6	2.6
TRAPPED OIL (nonflowing)	2.5	0–?
HEAVY OIL (tar sands)	5.0	0.5–2.5
UNCONVENTIONAL NATURAL GAS	10+	0.07–?
OIL SHALE		
(more than 40 liters per metric ton)	200	1.0–?
(less than 40 liters per metric ton)	10,000	?
1983 WORLD OIL AND GAS CONSUMPTION	0.018	
1983 WORLD ENERGY CONSUMPTION	0.03	

*1 metric ton of coal is taken to be equal to 27.2×10^9 joules.
 1 barrel of crude oil is taken to be equal to 6×10^9 joules.

FIG. 3-12 Rising concentration of carbon dioxide in the atmosphere as measured at an observatory on Mauna Loa, Hawaii. The yearly oscillation is due to the control exerted by the seasons on the cycle of photosynthesis and respiration in the northern hemisphere. (Data from *Geophysical Monitoring for Climate Change,* published by National Oceanic and Atmospheric Administration.)

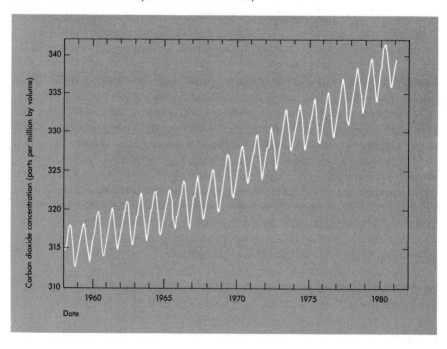

how to use. Second, oil and gas, the two fuels we have come to rely on most heavily, are the two least abundant. Their production, however, is also the least expensive in terms of manpower and disruption of the environment. Large-scale shifts to other fossil fuels will inevitably be accompanied by rising prices and many new problems, such as those of disruption of the land by large-scale mining and the need to develop new and larger systems of transportation. Fossil fuels share a common environmental problem that may eventually pose severe problems for us all—when they are burned, they release carbon dioxide to the atmosphere. If the release rate is slow, the excess carbon dioxide is taken up by plants through photosynthesis, or it dissolves in the ocean from which it is eventually precipitated as calcium carbonate; the composition of the atmosphere would thus remain unaffected. But we now burn fossil fuels, and release carbon dioxide, more rapidly than plants and the ocean can respond. As a result, the level of carbon dioxide in the atmosphere is rising slowly (Fig. 3-12). This may pose an environmental problem because of the interaction of carbon dioxide and electromagnetic radiation. Short-wavelength radiation coming from the sun passes through the atmosphere without influence from carbon dioxide. The sun's rays heat the land and sea, and the energy is then radiated back to space as long-wavelength radiation. Carbon dioxide retards the escape of the long-wavelength radiation, which causes the atmosphere to become warmer. This in turn leads to a slow warming of the world's climate. How such changes will influence local factors such as rainfall and agriculture remains conjectural.

One very clear conclusion that can be drawn is that we would be wise to turn increasingly to sources of energy that do not involve the mining and burning of fossil fuels. In the next chapter, therefore, other possible energy sources at the earth's surface will be discussed.

four

energy for the future

Energy is the sine qua non of a modern society's ability to do the things it wants to do. Such goals as maintaining the standard of living for a growing population, national security, improved quality of life, increased affluence and increased assistance to less developed societies can only be attained with increasingly large amounts of energy. While lower energy costs allow a society more freedom of action in seeking its goals, the availability of energy is the first requirement of having any freedom of action at all. (Report to the President of the United States, by Dixy Lee Ray, December, 1973.)

If supplies of fossil fuels are someday to be found wanting, and if use of the supplies have unacceptable environmental consequences, what will take their place? Dr. Ray's statement, quoted above, emphasizes the necessity for forthcoming answers. We do, of course, already draw energy from sources other than fossil fuels—sources such as wood, hydroelectric schemes, nuclear power plants, the sun, tidal power, windmills, and geothermal steam fields. But as discussed in Chapter 3, society has built such a massive dependence on fossil fuels that all other energy sources used today supply less than 10 percent of the total. By 1983 the peoples of the world had raised their consumption of energy to an estimated 3×10^{20} joules per year; the total continues to rise slowly. 3×10^{20} joules per year is a consumption rate of 9.5×10^{12} watts, which means that less than 1×10^{12} watts are now being drawn from sources other than oil, gas, and coal. If society is to be maintained, and if living standards in the less developed parts of the world are to be raised, it seems inevitable that the balance in fuel sources must ultimately shift away from such heavy dependence on fossil fuels. In this chapter, therefore, an attempt is made to put the magnitude of other fuel sources into perspective.

The Earth's Energy Flux

Before evaluating specific resources, let us consider the energy budget at earth's surface (Fig. 4-1). Energy reaches the earth's surface from three sources. The first source is the kinetic energy of the spinning earth. Part of the kinetic energy is available at earth's surface because ocean tides are a steady brake that is slowly stopping the rotation. Fortunately the rate of slowing is tiny—the length of a day increases by no more than a thousandth of a second a century—but it is fast enough so that 2.7×10^{12} watts of power is dissipated by the tides. Though tiny by comparison with other energy sources, the tides are, for all practical purposes, a renewable resource and certainly contain enough energy to merit attention.

The second source of energy comes from the earth's interior in the form of heat, commonly called geothermal heat, and it reaches the surface at a rate

FIG 4-1 Energy flow sheet for the surface of the earth. Energy reaches the surface from short wavelength radiation given off by the sun, from the rotation of the earth due to ocean tides, and by heat flowing out from the earth's interior. Because the temperature of the surface is constant, the energy radiated back into space must be just equal to the energy reaching the surface. (Adapted in part from M. K. Hubbert, 1962, Pub. 1000-D, Committee on Natural Resources, National Academy of Science.)

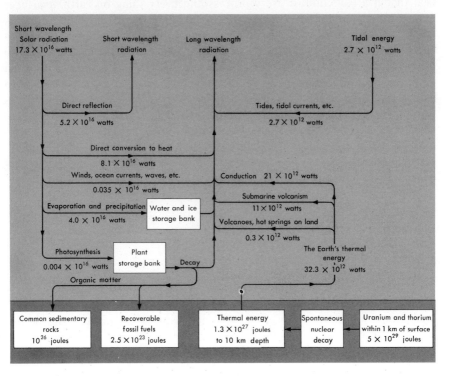

of 32.3 × 10^{12} watts. Some of earth's internal heat dates back to the violent processes that formed the earth billions of years ago, but the high temperatures inside the earth are maintained by heat given off during spontaneous disintegration of natural radioactive elements such as uranium and thorium. When the atomic disintegration process is artificially speeded up, as it is in nuclear power plants, the earth's supply of uranium and thorium becomes a nonrenewable resource of vast magnitude. The nuclear energy resource shown in Fig. 4-1 considers only the uranium and thorium in the upper 1 kilometer of the continents. The nuclear resource is enormous and can never be entirely used, not only because it is unthinkable that the entire land surface will be processed to a depth of a kilometer, but also because it requires more energy to recover the uranium and thorium from most rocks than can be usefully recovered in a nuclear power plant.

The third source is the sun, which warms the surface by heat and light. Solar energy reaches the earth at the rate of 1.5 × 10^{22} joules a day or, to put it in power terms, 17.3 × 10^{16} watts. This enormous flux of energy emphasizes an important point: *Energy is not in short supply. The questions to ask are how to use it and how to do so safely and responsibly.* Energy arriving from the sun is so vastly greater than the energy from the tides and earth's internal heat that it affects almost every process and every thing on earth's surface. Some of the incoming rays—about 30 percent—are simply reflected by clouds and by the earth's surface, but most rays pass into or through the atmosphere and follow the many paths shown in Fig. 4-1. By heating the atmosphere, the oceans, and the land, the sun's heat causes winds, rains, snowfalls, and ocean currents. Eventually, however, all of the energy is again radiated back into cold space, and the earth's surface remains in thermal balance. A small fraction of the solar-derived energy is temporarily stored in water reservoirs such as lakes and rivers. Another small fraction is stored in living plants and animals. Wood and hydroelectric energy from streams, therefore, are both renewable energy sources. Another much longer-term storage of solar energy occurs, as discussed in Chapter 3, when organic matter from dead plants and animals is trapped and buried in sediments as they go through the long rock cycle.

ENERGY FROM TIDES

Tides are a result of the gravitational pull of the moon and the sun. Of the two, the effect of the moon is by far the largest. We can picture two tidal bulges, one adjacent to the moon, a second counterbalancing it on the opposite side of the earth. As the earth spins on its axis, the bulges move and produce two high and two low tides everywhere each day. Tidal power, therefore, is an expression of the power of the earth's rotation. Tidal power is as large as it is because continents, islands, and shallow parts of the ocean act as barriers to the smooth passage of the tidal bulges.

This simple picture is complicated by effects from the sun and the irregular shape of the earth's surface. Tidal heights are not uniform everywhere. They rarely exceed a meter in the deep ocean, but over continental shelves they may reach 20 meters. Movement of such vast masses of water requires a great deal of energy; the total tidal power is estimated to be 2.7×10^{12} watts. Throughout a year, this amounts to 0.85×10^{20} joules.

Utilizing the rise and fall of tides presents many problems. Plants already generate electricity from tidal power in France on the River Rance, and in the U.S.S.R. on Kislaya Bay. These experiences demonstrate that tidal heights of 5 meters or more and easily dammed bays or estuaries are needed in order for tidal plants to operate effectively. Unfortunately, most coastal tides are about 2 meters high, and no more than 30 places around the world satisfy the right conditions. The most important are the Bay of Fundy in Canada and adjacent Passamaquoddy in the United States, the French coast along the English Channel (where the plant in the River Rance has operated successfully for many years), British river estuaries facing the Irish Sea, the White Sea coast in the U.S.S.R., and the Kimberly coast of northwestern Australia. If each site were fully developed, and if the schemes were so efficient that 20 percent of the local tidal energy could be recovered, the world's tidal power capacity would be 0.032×10^{12} watts—not much by comparison with our present-day needs, but very large for those few favored areas where high tides occur. Tidal power may well have an important, although local, future, because it seems to be one of the few energy systems that is without serious environmental drawbacks.

ENERGY FROM THE SOLID EARTH

Geothermal Energy

Anyone who has been down in a mine knows that rock temperatures increase with depth. Measurements made in deep drill holes from around the world show increases from 15°C to 75°C per kilometer; temperatures of 5,000°C or more are reached in the core. The size of the earth is so great that a vast amount of heat energy is stored within it.

Heat flows from a hot body to a cold one; thus, there is a slow outward flow of heat from the earth. The flow averages 6.3×10^{-6} joule per square centimeter per second or, to put it in power units, 32.3×10^{12} watts across the earth's entire surface. The total amount is vast, but very diffuse. If all the heat escaping from a square meter could somehow be gathered and used to heat a cup of water, it would take five days and nights to bring it to a boil.

Despite the steady loss of heat, the earth is cooling very slowly—so slowly, in fact, that it is impossible to measure the cooling over the life span of a human being. The reasons are twofold. First, the rocks of the earth are poor conductors of heat; outer layers act as thermal blankets for the hot interior. Second, new heat is added continually. Trace amounts of several naturally radioactive atoms, principally uranium-238,* uranium-235, thorium-232, and potassium-40, occur throughout the earth. Each time that a radioactive atom disintegrates a tiny amount of heat is released. Atoms in average igneous rock in the continental crust, for example, release 3.9×10^{-9} joule per gram of rock per day. This is not much heat, but, summed over the whole earth, it is sufficient to maintain a cooling rate that can be estimated to be no more than about 100°C every billion years. Clearly, earth's interior will continue to be hot for billions of years to come.

Assessing geothermal heat as a potential energy source is complex because it involves a definition problem. What exactly is meant by geothermal energy? We can't mean all the heat in the earth, because most of the earth's interior is inaccessible. If we limit our discussion to the upper 10 kilometers of the continental crust—because only one well in the U.S.S.R. has ever been drilled deeper, and because heat in the oceanic crust is only accessible from islands because of the covering ocean—it is a simple matter to calculate that all of the heat energy above the 10°C average temperature of earth's surface is an enormous 1.3×10^{27} joules. Geothermal heat is already used at a few favorable sites around the world, but how much more, if any, of this heat can be considered a potential fuel resource? And if it can, how can the heat be recovered, and at what cost? This is really a combined engineering and economic question, and it is the same question that arises each time a nonconventional source of energy is discussed. There seem to be two ways by which some of the heat might be recovered.

Approximately two-thirds of the heat now lost by the earth (a rate of 21×10^{12} watts) reaches the surface by conduction through rocks. Replacing rocks with better conductors—metal rods, for instance—would speed up the heat flow but seems a most unlikely step for us to take. The rest of the heat—11.3×10^{12} watts—reaches the surface by convection, a process by which hot, low-density fluids rise up through the cooler, denser rocks that enclose them. Magma, hot water, and steam are the most important convecting fluids, and they usually occur in close geographic association. This is so because magma brings abnormally hot rocks to shallow depths. Most of the convective heat reaches the surface along the midocean ridges—the estimated rate is 11×10^{12} watts—and seawater is the cooling medium. No one has yet suggested how submarine volcanic heat might be tapped, but we already know how to use volcanic heat on land. If a rock unit that is both porous and permeable hap-

---

*Uranium-238 designates an atom that contains 146 neutrons in addition to 92 protons for a total of 238 particles in its nucleus.

pens to be close to a shallow magma body intruded into the continental crust, it will become an underground reservoir for the steam and water heated by the magma (Fig. 4-2). The hot water and steam in the rock pores form what is sometimes misleadingly called a geothermal pool. If the "pool" contains rocks that are permeable, the hot water and steam can be drawn out through drill holes and used to drive electrical turbines. When the fluid is particularly hot, it will be steam; when it is less hot, it will be a mixture of steam and water or, as in most geothermal pools, simply hot water. Because steam is preferred for electricity-generating turbines, the only geothermal pools extensively developed so far contain steam. They are used in Iceland, Japan, Italy, Indonesia, the Philippines, U.S.S.R., U.S.A., and New Zealand, but many others are planned for future development. In a few places, geothermal hot water is already used for space heating, for swimming pools, and for agricultural hot houses, but even though such uses are growing rapidly, they are minor compared to generation of electricity.

Unfortunately, the convective heat flux through centers of volcanism on land is small, about 0.3×10^{12} watts. Experts from the U.S. Geological Survey report that down to a depth of 3 kilometers, which seems to be the limit for the occurrence of big geothermal pools in continental crust, the worldwide

FIG. 4-2 Geothermal reservoirs occur on land where a water-saturated, porous, and permeable rock unit becomes heated. Heating occurs most commonly in areas of present or recent past volcanic activity, such as the western United States, Japan, Mexico, Iceland, Italy, and New Zealand.

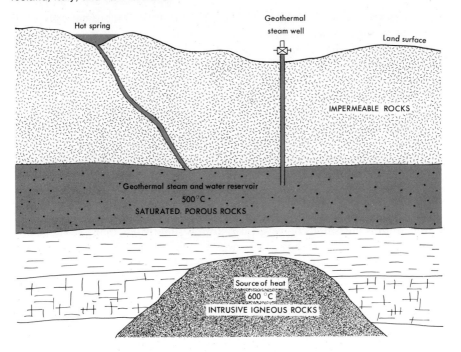

reserves of geothermal power are about 8×10^{19} joules. This seems a discouragingly small amount and suggests that geothermal energy, like tidal energy, will be important locally but will be minor on a global scale. The total heat energy in the pools is, of course, much larger than 8×10^{19} joules. But the estimate takes note of the low efficiency with which electricity can be generated from geothermal steam; experience in Iceland, New Zealand, and Italy suggests that no more than 1 percent of the energy in a pool can be effectively recovered.

We must also ask whether man-made geothermal pools might somehow be created so that the huge reservoir of heat in ordinary rocks might be tapped. Experiments to test this idea are already under way in the United States and France, and possibly in other countries. In the United States, the location of the experiment is the Jemez Mountains in New Mexico. Here, on the flanks of a recently extinct volcano, hot, dry rocks can be reached by drilling at reasonably shallow depths. Two holes have been drilled and the rocks between them fractured at depth by controlled explosions, thus creating the necessary porosity and permeability. Cool water is passed down one drill hole, is heated as it traverses the hot, fractured rock, and then is returned through the second hole. The same water is used again and again. So far the experiment has been only partly successful, because it has proved difficult to adequately control the rock fracture patterns, but the process has certainly proved technologically feasible. Whether or not it can be made cost-effective is a question for the future.

Reserves of geothermal energy in natural reservoirs represent only a tiny fraction of all geothermal heat. Experts cannot agree how much of the remainder in hot, dry rocks should be considered a potential resource. The amount considered recoverable depends on one's optimism for future technological advances. Readers can choose for themselves. This writer tends to be skeptical that we will ever get much energy from hot, dry rocks, and therefore he places the potential resources at 10^{20} joules, about the same level as the reserves in geothermal pools.

Nuclear Fission Energy

Nuclear energy arises from a process first deciphered by Albert Einstein, who showed in 1905 that matter and energy can be converted from one to the other. Atomic nuclei are built up from neutrons and protons. When the mass of an atom is measured, however, it is always slightly less than the sum of the masses of individual protons and neutrons. Helium, for example, contains two protons and two neutrons and should weigh 4.04403 atomic mass units. In fact, helium only weighs 4.00260 units. The missing mass was converted to energy when the particles joined together to form the nucleus.

Disaggregation of the nucleus into all of its constituent pieces can only occur through the addition of enough energy to replace the missing mass. The missing mass therefore acts as a sort of glue to hold the particles together and is called the *binding energy* of the nucleus. Binding energy per proton or neutron in the nucleus varies with the total mass of the atom (Fig. 4-3). The lower an atom sits on the binding energy curve, the more energy is released when it is formed from its constituent particles.

Because there is a trough in the binding energy curve, it can be seen from Fig. 4-3 that two kinds of processes will release nuclear energy. First, there is the *fusion* of light elements, such as hydrogen and lithium, to form heavier elements. This is the process that goes on in the sun and in hydrogen bombs. Although fusion has not yet been achieved in the laboratory under conditions such that the energy produced exceeds the energy used, some scientists believe that success will be achieved and that fusion might be a principal energy source for the future. Second, there is the transformation, or *fission,* of heavy elements, such as uranium or thorium, not into the constituent protons and neutrons, but into two or more intermediate-weight atoms sitting lower on the binding energy curve. Fission is the process that occurs in the atom bomb. Because the reaction can be controlled, fission has already been used for the generation of electricity by nuclear power plants. We will therefore consider fission-released energy first.

Some radioactive elements can be made to fission when neutrons are fired into the nucleus, making the atoms unstable and subject to spontaneous disintegration. If neutrons are also released by the disintegration process, a sustained, or chain, disintegration can occur. The only naturally occurring fissionable atom is uranium-235, which comprises 0.7 percent of all natural uranium atoms. The uranium-235 chain reaction was first achieved by Pro-

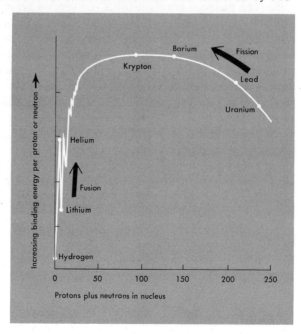

FIG. 4-3 Binding energy, produced by conversion of some of the mass of each proton and neutron in an atomic nucleus, varies with the number of protons and neutrons. The lower an atom sits on the curve, the more energy will be given off when protons and neutrons combine to form its nucleus. Arrows indicate direction of movement along the binding energy curve during fusion and fission.

fessor Enrico Fermi on December 2, 1942, in one of the most important experiments ever performed.

The cost of separating uranium-235 atoms from the more common uranium-238 atoms is high. Once separated, however, the disintegration of a single atom releases 3.2×10^{-11} joule of energy; because 1 gram of uranium-235 contains 2.56×10^{21} atoms, fission of a gram of uranium produces 8.19×10^{10} joules—equivalent to the energy released when 2.7 metric tons of coal are burned. Many uranium-235 power plants are now generating electricity. By 1980, 186 nuclear power plants were producing electricity in 20 countries. Many of the plants had more than one reactor, and both the number of active reactors and the countries where they are installed is rising all the time. This is so despite the fact that contracts to build new nuclear plants in the United States were being cancelled as this book was being completed, in addition to the fact that some already completed plants in the United States have been denied operating licenses due to faulty construction. The total power capacity of 1980's 186 plants was reported to be 110×110^9 watts, sufficient to provide 7.6 percent of the world's electrical power. Among the users of nuclear power plants, the United States is reported to have the largest power capacity with 45.5 percent of the total, followed by Europe with 28 percent, and Japan with 11.8 percent.

There are many important questions facing operators of uranium-235 plants. One is economics—can the uranium fuel be produced less expensively than equivalent amounts of coal or oil can be, and can power plants be constructed cheaply enough to be competitive with coal or oil plants? The richest mines can produce uranium for a few cents a gram. Because uranium-235 is only 0.7 percent of the mass, the base cost of uranium-235 without any allowance for the difficult and expensive separation of uranium-235 from uranium-238 is in excess of $3.00 a gram. The coal equivalent of a gram of uranium-235 is at least $15.00 from the least expensive mines. Uranium separation costs are not made public by the United States and other governments that carry out the process, because much of the separations is carried out for production of weapons. Apparently, however, costs are less than the $12.00 a gram difference between uranium and the equivalent in coal, so uranium-235 is presently an economically competitive fuel. The economics of plant construction are less clear. Twenty years of experience have led to increasing rather than decreasing costs, because engineers have run into more and more unexpected problems. As a result, many contracts for plant installations have been delayed or cancelled in recent years.

Side-by-side with the economic questions are issues of safety that many people perceive to be the most troubling problems of all. If a nuclear power plant fails for some unexpected reason and releases radioactive materials into the environment, the consequences could be disastrous. Fortunately, no major disasters have yet occurred, but there have been some close calls and the potential is certainly there. Even more troubling than plant safety, however, is the problem of safe disposal of the radioactive wastes from the spent fuel. The wastes remain toxic for hundreds of years and must be buried in disposal sites in such a way that no radioactive debris can escape into the groundwater, the atmosphere, or the biosphere. Although geologists can point to many places where natural accumulations of radioactive elements remain safely bottled up in rocks, the human record for safe disposal of wastes, such as toxic wastes from chemical plants, is hardly a matter for pride and confidence. Assuming that fears can be allayed and that the needed technological advances can be made so that nuclear power can move safely ahead, what is the picture for fuel reserves?

The presently installed uranium-235 power plants will reportedly severely strain known reserves of rich uranium deposits by the year 2000, though how much of the strain arises from weapons use is not reported. This has led many countries to look at nuclear alternatives. There are two obvious alternatives that involve more abundant materials than uranium-235. Uranium-238 and thorium-232 are the obvious alternatives, because they are much more abundant than uranium-235 and can both be converted into fissionable atoms. When a neutron with the right velocity hits the nucleus of a uranium-238 atom, it is absorbed, causing two electrons to be emitted and the atom to be converted to plutonium-239. Similarly, thorium-232 can be converted to uranium-233. Both plutonium-239 and uranium-233 are fissionable and can sustain chain reactions. The trick, therefore, is to balance production of neutrons from fissioning so that the conversion of uranium-238 or thorium-232 equals or exceeds the rate at which the fissioning atoms are used up. This process is called *breeding,* and the device in which it occurs is called a *breeder reactor* (Fig. 4-4). The same amount of heat is produced from uranium-238 and thorium-232 reactions as from uranium-235. But with breeder reactors, the cost of the fuel becomes insignificant: At 1983 prices, the cost of raw uranium for a breeder reactor is equivalent to coal at 2 cents a metric ton or to oil at less than half a cent a barrel. Certain common rocks and even seawater could

FIG. 4-4 Schematic diagram showing the difference between the uranium-235 (U^{235}) fission reactions and the uranium-238 (U^{238}) transformation into plutonium-239 (Pu^{239}) and subsequent plutonium fission. Heat produced in both kinds of reactions can be converted to electricity.

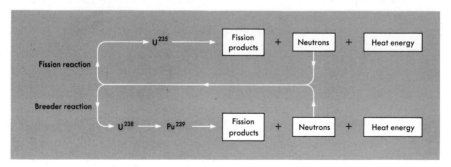

possibly be used as sources of uranium, and the fuel would still be competitive with coal and oil. For this reason, research on breeder reactors has been very active, and some experts believe that they will be operating commercially by the year 1995. They are already operating on an experimental but nevertheless power-producing basis in France, Canada, the United Kingdom, and the U.S.S.R. Unfortunately, the engineering and safety problems posed by breeder reactors are even greater than those posed by uranium-235 plants.

Most of the work on atomic energy has centered on uranium reactions, so it is uranium that has been most actively exploited and explored. Uranium occurs in two valence states, U^{+4} and U^{+6}, and the interplay of these governs its distribution in the crust. In certain igneous rocks, uranium is widespread as UO_2, the mineral uraninite (sometimes called pitchblende), which has uranium in the U^{+4} state. UO_2 is practically insoluble, but if the U^{+4} is oxidized to U^{+6}, as occurs under certain conditions at the earth's surface, the complex uranyl ion $(UO_2)^{+2}$ is formed; this ion can form separate compounds that are soluble. A compound such as uranyl carbonate facilitates the solution and movement of uranium in surface waters. Precipitation occurs when the solutions encounter a reducing agent, such as organic matter, that returns the uranium to the U^{+4} state and again forms less soluble compounds. The reduced uranium may precipitate as UO_2 or $USiO_4$, as it has done in many of the famous Colorado Plateau deposits where buried logs have been found almost completely replaced by uraninite, and as it has done in many of the organic-rich shales around the world, such as the 100,000 square kilometers of Chattanooga Shale in Alabama and Kentucky, and in the Alum Shale of Sweden and Norway. Finally, the uranium may be taken up by another mineral; the mineral in which this occurs most commonly is apatite, $Ca_5(PO_4)_3(OH,F)$, with U^{+4} atoms entering the crystal structure of apatite. This is apparently the manner by which uranium is concentrated in the Florida phosphate deposits.

The measured resources of uranium in rich deposits are unfortunately not as large as we might hope. During the years from 1945 to 1960, uranium received the most intensive mineralogical and geological scrutiny ever accorded a metal. A great many rich deposits were located and, following the assumption that further prospecting would locate yet more high-grade deposits, confident and rosy predictions were made of large, easily won potential resources. Further work suggests that this confidence was misplaced. A renewal of intense prospecting, commencing in the late 1960's and continuing through much of the 1970's, was not as successful in locating the hoped-for bonanzas in the United States, but it did lead to the discovery of some exceedingly large and rich deposits in Australia, Canada, and Namibia.

The richest deposits in the United States are apparently secondary concentrations in sedimentary rocks, arising from the movement of uranium by groundwater. The largest and most numerous deposits are found in rocks of the Jurassic and Triassic periods in the Colorado Plateau of western Colorado, eastern Utah, northeastern Arizona, and northwestern New Mexico. Other rich deposits in sedimentary rocks, but from the Cenozoic, are found in Wyoming and Texas. All of these deposits, together with smaller and less valuable occurrences in numerous other states, account for a reserve of uranium reported by the International Atomic Energy Agency to be only 708,000 metric tons (Table 4-1). The reserves reported for Canada are principally located in rich deposits in the Great Bear Lake region, Northwest Territories, and in the Blind River district north of Lake Huron in Ontario, where extensive sedimentary rocks of Precambrian age contain disseminated uranium minerals of detrital origin. Large South African reserves are associated with the Witwatersrand gold deposits, where trace amounts of uranium, also of detrital origin, are recovered as a by-product of gold production. The Australian reserves are in deposits of several different kinds, one of which is said to be the richest kind of deposit ever discovered.

Reserves of rich uranium ores in the non-Communist world are not large. The figures are probably conservative, however, because an element of secrecy and caution surrounds a strategic commodity like uranium. Regardless of how much the reserves are understated, however, they are certainly not large enough to support extensive use of uranium-235 power stations very far into the future. Let us consider, for example, what would happen if all of the reserves and resources listed in Table 4-1 were used solely for their uranium-235 content. If the conversion of heat energy to electricity was 40 percent efficient, the total energy produced would only be 8×10^{20} joules. On the other hand,

Table 4-1 Estimated uranium resources in ores rich enough to be mined for use in uranium-235 power plants, together with estimated rates of production for 1990. Data are reported as the oxide, U_3O_8. No distinctions are drawn between reserves and resources, and no data are reported by the Communist countries.

Country	Reasonably assured resources. (Metric tons of U_3O_8)	Estimated production rate, 1990.* (Metric tons of U_3O_8 per year)
Australia[†]	1,600,000	9,000
U.S.A.[†]	894,000	6,000
Rep. of South Africa[‡]	391,000	6,000
Canada[‡]	235,000	13,000
Niger[‡]	160,000	?
Namibia[‡]	133,000	4,000
France[‡]	55,300	?
Other[‡]	608,000	5,000

*Production rate estimate from *Mining Annual Review*, 1983.

[†]Resource data from *Am. Assoc. of Petroleum Geologists, Bulletin* v. 67, p. 1999–2008, 1983.

[‡]Resource data from *Mining Annual Review*, 1980. Much of the large "Other" category is in low-grade deposits in Sweden.

if the same efficiency factor was used for all the uranium-238 in a breeder reactor, the available energy total soars to 1140×10^{20} joules.

Beyond the rich deposits, it is difficult to make an assessment; the necessary work simply has not been done. Within the United States a general evaluation has been made of the kinds of source materials available (Fig. 4-5), and an estimate was made that if costs rose as high as $1.00 a gram, about 2×10^9 metric tons of uranium could be recovered. This enormous mass could produce 6.6×10^{25} joules of electricity. Similar figures pertain in other parts of the world. Reserve estimates for thorium are less certain than are those for uranium. Because thorium is a more abundant element than uranium in the continental crust, it is possible that its potential resources exceed those of uranium. Provided that the necessary technological developments can be made to make breeder reactors safe and free from failure, therefore, nuclear fission energy would appear to have a very bright future. However, there is still the major problem of nuclear waste disposal to be resolved. Most of the wastes are highly radioactive but, unfortunately, have little or no practical use, so they must be safely disposed in an acceptable waste depository. Because some of the radioactive wastes remain dangerous for hundreds and even thousands of years, the question of disposal sites is a politically sensitive one. Most sci-

FIG. 4-5 Long-term, but low-grade, resources of uranium occur in phosphate deposits, lignites, and black shales. Richer deposits, for which present reserves can be estimated, occur mostly in and around a region known as the Colorado Plateau. (After M. K. Hubbert, Energy Resources, Pub. 1000-D, Committee on Natural Resources, National Academy of Sciences—National Research Council, Washington, D.C., 1962.)

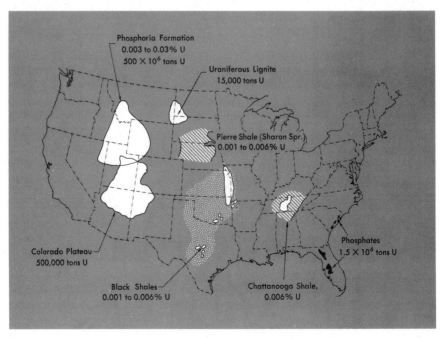

entists and engineers who have studied the problem conclude that safe burial sites can be prepared and safe burial containers fabricated. Communities near proposed burial sites may not draw the same conclusions, however. So far, no country has found a solution that is acceptable to everyone, so radioactive waste products are being held in temporary containers on the surface, which is, unfortunately, the most dangerous, vulnerable, and least acceptable solution.

Nuclear Fusion Energy

While we know how to use fission, we have not yet learned how to use energy from fusion. When we have learned, however, fusion reactions will open the way to use of nonrenewable energy resources that really are astronomic in magnitude.

The greatest amount of energy comes from fusion of the lightest element, hydrogen, to produce helium, a reaction that produces most of the energy emitted by the sun. Similar reactions involving heavier elements produce lesser yields of energy as the masses increase but, on the other hand, they are easier to control. The main reaction in the H-bomb, for example, involves fusion of two atoms of deuterium (a form of hydrogen with 1 neutron and 1 proton in the nucleus) to form helium. Each time this combination occurs, 7.9×10^{-13} joule of energy are released. Each cubic centimeter of seawater contains approximately 10^{16} atoms of deuterium, and because the volume of the oceans is 1.35×10^{24} cubic centimeters, the fusion potential of deuterium in the sea is 10.7×10^{27} joules.

Hydrogen fusion, when it is attained, promises the use of an even larger resource because there are 6,500 hydrogen atoms for every deuterium atom in the sea. With such large numbers, it becomes obvious why many authorities believe that extensive research into fusion reactions should continue to be supported. Success with fusion energy, regardless of whether deuterium or hydrogen is used, is clearly not limited by fuel resources.

ENERGY FROM THE SUN

Solar energy has positive features that are not combined in any other source. It is renewable, it is clean, it is dependable, and it is of such great magnitude that it exceeds by thousands of times the amount of supplementary energy we use today or are likely to use in the future. We already use solar energy in many ways, of course; greenhouses, sunrooms in houses, and light wells into the dark interiors of large buildings are examples. It seems certain that such passive uses of solar energy will increase greatly in the future. The major challenge lies not with passive heating systems but rather with so-called active solar systems in which solar heat is stored for later use or is used directly to drive an engine or to generate electricity. Here too, many devices have already been invented, but most are inefficient and expensive to build. The inefficiency arises because most devices first heat water or a similar liquid, and this, in turn, is used to heat a house or to drive a motor or an electrical generator. Recent research on devices called photovoltaic cells, which convert solar radiation directly to electricity, suggests that conversion efficiencies of 30 percent might someday be attained. Photovoltaic cells are already used for certain special functions, but they are expensive and are not presently competitive with conventional power plants. Furthermore, because solar rays are so diffuse at the earth's surface, it can be calculated that about 8 square kilometers of collecting surface would be necessary for a power plant producing 10^9 watts—about the capacity of today's larger nuclear power plants. The costs of the plants, the large collection areas needed, and the high percentages of cloudy days in many areas, particularly those in high latitudes, will probably prevent entire countries from ever using solar power alone. But for areas fortunate enough to enjoy relatively cloudless skies, solar power is without doubt the most attractive possibility for the future.

Water Power

Solar energy need not be collected directly. Figure 4-1 shows that about 23 percent of the incoming solar radiation is used in evaporating the water that falls as rain and snow. In effect, the sun acts as a great pump, raising water from the sea and dumping it on the land, from which it runs downhill into the sea. Thus, running water is activated by solar energy and is a renewable resource.

Water power has been used in small ways for thousands of years, but it was only at about the beginning of the twentieth century that large-scale damming of rivers commenced for generation of electricity. Hydropower is now the most highly developed of all the renewable energy resources. Evaluation of energy resources from running water involves an assessment of the amount of water flowing in streams and rivers and of how far downhill it flows before reaching the sea. Using data collected by the U.S. Geological Survey, F. L. Adams in 1962 calculated that the power present in water that runs off continents is 2.9×10^{12} watts (Table 4-2). Not all of this is usable. Flow rates vary tremendously in the course of a year, and it is not feasible to dam a river completely. In 1981, the United Nations Environment Programme reported their estimates of the power actually recoverable by considering all feasible dam sites (Table 4-2). As with geothermal and tidal power, the amount recoverable is a small fraction of the total available.

Two points are of paramount importance in consideration of water power. The first, which is an unfavorable point, is that even if the world's community will accept the total damming of its great river systems, the dams have definite and rather short lifetimes. A moving stream of water carries a load of fine mud particles in suspension; this material starts to be deposited

Table 4-2 Water-power capacity around the world.

	Total runoff potential* (watts)	Recoverable potential† (watts)	Recoverable potential developed (percent)
Asia and Europe	10.8×10^{11}	2.2×10^{11}	44.6
Africa	7.8×10^{11}	1.3×10^{11}	4.3
South and Central America	5.8×10^{11}	0.75×10^{11}	27.2
North America	3.1×10^{11}	0.66×10^{11}	75.2
Oceania	1.1×10^{11}	0.11×10^{11}	30.5

*From F. L. Adams after M. K. Hubbert, 1969.
†From "The World Environment, 1972–1982." A report by the United Nations Environment Programme, 1982.

as soon as the stream is dammed and the velocity drops. Depending on how much sediment the stream carries, a reservoir can be completely filled by sediment in periods ranging from 50 to 200 years. The great Aswan Dam on the Nile, for example, will be at least half silted up by the year 2025 because the Nile is a very muddy river. Water power may be renewable, but the water power sites are nonrenewable, because the volume of silt to be removed from a major reservoir is so huge that it is impractical to consider doing so. The second point, which is a favorable one, can be seen from Table 4-2. The world's largest undeveloped potential lies in South America and Africa. Inasmuch as these continents have small coal resources, it is fortunate that their water power is so plentiful. The long-term future for water power in the Southern Hemisphere must be considered very promising.

Wind and Ocean Power

If we refer again to Fig. 4-1, we see that about 46 percent of incoming solar energy is absorbed by the oceans, the land, and the atmosphere. This energy, in addition to producing winds, waves, and ocean currents, warms the seas and produces all of our weather patterns. At least some of it can be considered a potential resource. Estimates of the total global wind power are very large—on the order of 10^{15} watts—but much of the power is in high altitude winds and is not recoverable by devices on the land surface. Steady surface winds, such as the trade winds, have a power level of about 10^{12} watts, and some of this power can be recovered by using windmills. Unfortunately, wind power systems have undesirable environmental impacts. They are unsightly, often noisy, and, in case of failure, very dangerous. Furthermore, it can be estimated that the cost of erecting large windmills at sea or along the shore in order to generate electricity is so great that the power produced would cost several times more than would power from other sources. For smaller-scale uses, as in transportation at sea, for recreation, and in farm use, however, wind power has long had many uses. Many experts predict a resurgence of windmills and other small-scale devices in the future.

When the sun warms the ocean by heating its surface, a thermal gradient occurs (Fig. 4-6). It is theoretically possible to draw on the ocean's vast heat reservoir by using the gradient, much as hot water is used from geothermal schemes. The difficulty is the small temperature difference involved—no more than 20°C, even in the tropics. Nevertheless, a small pilot plant using ocean thermal power was built and run for a short time by French engineers near Abidjan on the West African coast after World War II. From this experiment, larger schemes have been devised, engineers have been granted patents, and a successful experimental plant has been run in the waters off Hawaii. No one has yet convinced either private or governmental investors that larger schemes are economical, however. If they ever do, another astronomically large source of energy will be made available. Just how large is difficult to estimate, because it depends on the efficiency of the generating plant. Even if it was less

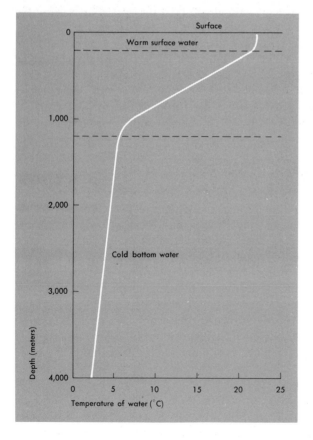

FIG. 4-6 A generalized representation of the vertical temperature distribution in the ocean. Scientists have proposed several devices for using the temperature difference between warm surface and cold bottom waters as a means of using some of the ocean's thermal energy.

than 1 percent, the ocean's thermal energy potential exceeds the potential from fossil fuels. Perhaps it is not even necessary to use electrical generation. Scientists have already proposed and tried some imaginative schemes; one involves the preservation of foods such as flour and corn at the near freezing temperature of the ocean floor; another involves the pumping of cold ocean water for use in tropical air conditioning systems. Such uses would at least help ease the strain on fossil fuels.

Another expression of heat energy in the oceans is the great surface currents. The Gulf Stream, for example, has mechanical power from its flow that is equal to 2.2×10^{14} watts, or 7×10^{21} joules per year. But how such a vast renewable resource could be harnessed lies in the realm of speculation. It has been proposed, for example, that a huge turbine encased in an open tube would turn and could be used to generate electricity if the tube were anchored to the seafloor in such a way that part of the Gulf Stream would flow through. Strange as this scheme sounds, engineering feasibility tests have been made and experiments are underway to test the idea.

Waves are yet another expression of solar energy. Waves arise from winds blowing over the ocean, and they contain energy that is many thousands of times greater than that in tides. For example, a single wave that is 1.8 meters high and moving in water 9 meters deep generates approximately 10^4 watts for each meter of wave front. What vast amounts of energy are expended daily on the shorelines of the world! Wave power has been used to ring bells and blow whistles as a navigational aid for many years, but only recently has large-scale power production been considered. The possibilities do not seem too encouraging. One patented scheme uses troughs covered with a flexible film and filled with hydraulic fluid. When the flexible trough is placed on the seafloor, the weight of a passing wave forces the hydraulic fluid through a network of pipes and into a motor, which, in turn, drives a generator. Another involves a series of floating rafts joined by hinges. The rafts rock up and down as waves pass, and the rocking motion can be used to power mechanical devices of various sorts.

Biological Energy Sources

Plant matter can be burned as fuel or processed to make alcohol, methane, or some other combustible chemical compound. Since plants depend on sunlight for photosynthesis, the *biomass* is yet another expression of solar power. Estimates of the dry weight of all living plant matter on earth's land surface vary but average about 2×10^{12} metric tons. The annual growth rate, also expressed in dry weight, is about 0.15×10^{12} metric tons. If all of the annual growth were burned for fuel, we would recover energy many (eight to ten) times larger than our present energy consumption. It is clearly impossible to do this, because forests would have to be decimated, plant foods could not be eaten, and the drain on the soil would be tremendous. Controlled cropping of fuel plants, however, could certainly increase the amount of biomass that could be used as a fuel. In many parts of the world experiments are already underway to develop this obvious energy source. The results are likely to be more useful for tropical regions such as Brazil than for countries in the temperate zones where most of the world's food is grown. Even in temperate zones, however, agricultural and urban wastes could be used as fuel if the right sort of power plants were installed.

We should not be too skeptical about the use of solar energy resources. While the possibilities seem limited today, technologies of the future may change the whole picture. If ever a field of study beckoned persons with inventive genius, it is the whole field of solar power.

THE FUTURE

There is neither an energy crisis nor an energy shortage. There are vast amounts of energy, more than we could ever use. Crises related to the scarcity of fuels are of our own making: We have relied too heavily on two inexpensive fossil fuels, and as a result there is a petroleum crisis. As Chapters 3 and 4 demonstrate, there are many alternatives to oil and gas, and most offer the comforting side benefit of larger resources. But each alternative has drawbacks, too. Mining of coal, oil shale, and tar sand, for example, causes serious disruptions to the land surface; in addition, the burning of these fuels will continue the buildup of carbon dioxide in the atmosphere. Nuclear energy, the most obvious energy source on the horizon, also brings problems of heroic proportions. As previously discussed, wastes from nuclear power plants remain lethally radioactive for periods up to thousands of years. Can we dispose of them so that people thousands of years hence will not be threatened? We must protect generations at least as far into the future as the Romans are in our past. There is still another inescapable problem concerning breeder reactors: They produce more and more fissionable materials that can be used for nuclear weapons. Surely breeder reactors will increase the number of nuclear weapons and hence the likelihood of nuclear war.

Yet another problem must be faced if power plants—regardless of fuel—are to be made larger and larger. What is to be done with the waste heat that is generated? At present most plants send the waste heat to the atmosphere, thus influencing the local climate, or they use cooling water that is returned to streams and lakes, thereby raising the temperatures of local waterways. As plants grow large, so will the waste heat problem—unless innovative uses for it can be developed. Other problems concern the source of capital needed to finance vast power plants and the threat that exists when huge communities are dependent on plants that are vulnerable to strikes and attacks.

Changing energy sources will inevitably bring changes in life-styles. Fossil fuels are chemicals that can be easily transported and used in small quantities. Alternate energy sources can, in some cases, be converted to conveniently transported fuels such as hydrogen, but conversion is inefficient and expensive. Inevitably, therefore, energy use, such as that in our present systems of transportation, will change.

How the story will develop is part of the intriguing future. There are only two points about this future that now seem to be certain. Energy needs will continue to rise for at least the near future, and energy sources will slowly change. As sources change, so will machines using the energy, and so too will the demand patterns for metals to build the machines. We next turn, therefore, to metallic mineral resources.

the abundant metals

I have for many years been impressed with the steady depletion of our iron ore supply. It is staggering to learn that our once-supposed ample supply of rich ores can hardly outlast the generation now appearing, leaving only the leaner ores for the later years of the century. It is my judgment, as a practical man accustomed to dealing with those material factors on which our national prosperity is based, that it is time to take thought for the morrow. (Andrew Carnegie, Proceedings of a Conference of Governors in the White House, Washington, D.C., May 13–15, 1908.)

Metals have properties such as malleability, ductility, and high thermal and electrical conductivities. Metals are essential for technology; without metals, we could not have developed the remarkably diversified society in which we live. Indeed, the metalwinning and metalworking skills of an ancient community are sometimes used as one measure of its development; most of us are familiar with such terms as the Bronze Age and the Iron Age.

Metals can be divided into two classes on the basis of their abundance in the continental crust: the *scarce metals,* with abundances less than 0.1 percent; and the *abundant metals*—iron, aluminum, manganese, magnesium, and titanium—with abundances greater than 0.1 percent.

Almost every rock contains detectable amounts of each abundant metal; they are usually present in separate minerals rich in the individual elements. The chemical properties of the specific minerals determine whether or not a given rock can be considered a resource of an abundant metal. The first key factor is the ease with which a mineral containing an abundant metal can be physically separated from the valueless associated minerals. Concentration of a valuable mineral (also referred to as *beneficiation*) can be accomplished in several ways. The second key factor is the ease with which the mineral concentrate can be broken down chemically to release the metal. This can also be accomplished in several different ways and is generally referred to as *smelting*. The winning of a metal from a rock, therefore, consists of three separate steps—mining, beneficiation, and smelting. Abundant metals are usually combined with silicon and oxygen, the two most abundant elements of the crust, to form silicate minerals such as albite ($NaAlSi_3O_8$), anorthite ($CaAl_2Si_2O_8$), and garnet ($Mg_3Al_2Si_4O_{12}$). There is no difficulty presented by the mining or beneficiation of silicate minerals, but the smelting process is prohibitively difficult because it is very energy-intensive. The minerals in which the abundant metals are preferentially sought, therefore, are those from which the metals are most easily recovered by smelting: oxides and hydroxides, such as *magnetite* (Fe_3O_4), *hematite* (Fe_2O_3) and *gibbsite* (H_3AlO_3), and carbonates, such as *siderite* ($FeCO_3$) and *magnesite* ($MgCO_3$). Unfortunately, the desirable minerals are much less common than silicates, so the readily recovered fraction of any metal in the crust is tiny compared to the whole. Although not expressed in these words, it was this very point that drew Andrew Carnegie's concern in the quotation at the beginning of this chapter.

CONSUMPTION OF THE ABUNDANT METALS

Abundant metals have such high average concentrations in the crust that relatively small enrichments lead to valuable ores. Richness of a deposit is important, therefore, but if the correct minerals are not present, it is not a sufficient factor for recovery of abundant metals. This property stands in distinct contrast to the scarce metals discussed in Chapter 6. Time has shown that Andrew Carnegie's fears can be allayed. Rich ores are certainly desirable, but as long as the right minerals are present, quite lean ores can be beneficiated to very rich concentrates.

Abundant metals deserve their name on three accounts: abundance with the crust, magnitude of our consumption, and rate at which consumption is increasing (Fig. 5-1). Consumption is especially high for iron, the production of which exceeds the aggregate of all other metals. Because supplies are plentiful and production large, the cost of abundant metals is relatively low. In 1981, for example, the price of pig iron, the least expensive iron product, was about 13 cents a kilogram, of aluminum 135 cents, and of magnesium 275 cents. By comparison, three scarce metals, tin, tungsten, and rhodium, respectively, cost 1612 cents, 3300 cents, and 2,253,000 cents a kilogram. Despite the ready availability of ores, the processing of abundant metals requires advanced technology, and a great deal of energy. It is not surprising, therefore, that technologically advanced countries process and consume the largest fraction of each metal. In many cases, however, the ores and concentrates that are processed originate in countries that are not technologically advanced.

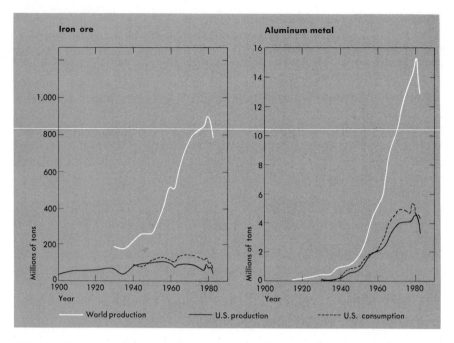

FIG. 5-1 World and U.S. production of two abundant metals. Iron is reported in the form of the ore in which it is mined because the ore is processed into different end products such as steel, pig iron, and various alloys. The content of iron recovered from the ore is approximately 50 percent by weight or more. The U.S., with six percent of the world's population, consumes a much larger percentage of the world production in each case, a pattern that holds true for many mineral commodities. However, the increasing divergence between the U.S. consumption curve and the world production curve reflects a rising standard of living around the world. Note the dramatic effect of the worldwide economic recession of the late 1970's and early 1980's on the production and use of both metals. (After U.S. Bureau of Mines.)

IRON

Iron, the second most abundant metal in the crust, is the backbone of civilization; it accounts for more than 95 percent of all metals consumed. A significant proportion of the remainder—nickel, chromium, molybdenum, tungsten, vanadium, cobalt, and manganese—are mined principally to be added to iron to produce steels, which have more of the desirable properties of strength and resistance to corrosion.

The smelting of iron from its oxide ores is a chemically simple process called *reduction*. A reducing agent such as carbon (usually in the form of coke made by expelling the gaseous fraction from bituminous coal) reacts with iron oxide at high temperatures to form metallic iron and carbon dioxide. Because iron ore is rarely pure, limestone ($CaCO_3$) must also be added as a flux to remove impurities by making a slag. Selection of the best ore and production of sufficiently high temperatures are technological problems, and the long history of smelting iron ores is the story of their solution. For more than 2000 years, until the beginning of the fourteenth century, all iron was produced in primitive forges by firing a charge of charcoal made from wood, iron ore, and limestone in a blast of air. These forges, remnants of which can still be found in parts of Africa and a form of which was used by the people of China during the late 1960's when they tried to boost their iron production in backyard furnaces, were small and capable of reducing the iron oxide to metallic iron but incapable of melting the reduced iron. They instead formed a welded mass of incandescent iron grains from which slag and other impurities were removed by vigorous hammering to form *wrought iron*.

As demand for iron increased, forges were made larger, and stronger air blasts were required to fire them. As a consequence, higher temperatures were reached and iron was produced in a molten form in furnaces that were forerunners of the modern blast furnace (Fig. 5-2). By the fourteenth century, *pig iron* (as the raw furnace product is called) was being produced in large quantities, and the foundations of the modern iron industry were laid. One addi-

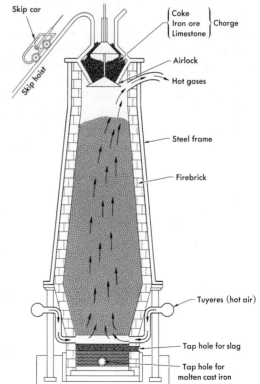

FIG. 5-2 Diagrammatic representation of the interior of a blast furnace. The production of each metric ton of pig iron from an ore containing 60 percent iron requires approximately 250 kilograms of limestone as a flux and a metric ton of coking coal. Electrical and oxygen furnaces require different mixes and are noteworthy for being more efficient in their use of coke, but the same three ingredients are used. The production of iron illustrates how interdependent are the uses of the different metals.

tional and very important step involved understanding how to make steel from iron. Steel is an alloy in which iron is the principal ingredient. The earliest and still most widely used steel is an alloy of iron and a small amount of carbon. Just the right amount of carbon imparts great strength, ductility, and tempering properties, which makes steel far more useful than iron. Steels of more recent origin, each with its own special properties, involve the alloying of iron with metals such as vanadium, tungsten, and molybdenum. Subsequent discoveries led to inexpensive ways to produce large quantities of high-grade steels from pig iron; more efficient blast furnace procedures, including the use of coke made from coal to replace charcoal from dwindling supplies of wood; other methods to reduce iron ores; methods of handling ores containing deleterious impurities such as phosphorus and sulphur; and methods of processing low-grade ores as the richest were used up. Many sophisticated developments occurred in the nineteenth century, laying the basis for today's technology in which all types of iron ores can be successfully handled, thus assuring the availability of truly enormous reserves. These developments have answered Andrew Carnegie's fears concerning supplies, but in return they have made transportation costs and access to markets greater factors in the production of iron than they are for any other metal.

Because the production of steel (and hence of the pig iron from which it is made) is large, the tonnage of additional materials is also large. Historically, this meant that the most profitable ores were those for which transportation costs were lowest. Britain's rise as the world's leading steel-producing country in the last century was due to the close proximity of high grade coal deposits and rich iron ores. In North America, construction of the St. Mary's River Canal at Sault Ste. Marie in 1855 opened the inexpensive water route of the Great Lakes, and made the largest and richest iron ores then known, those of the Mesabi Range in Minnesota, easily accessible to the rich Pennsylvanian coking coal deposits. As a result, Pittsburgh became the center of the iron-smelting industry and the United States began its rise as a leader among the world's iron and steel producers.

The transportation factor is still important, and now that large, world-wide systems of transportation have been developed, any country can have a steel industry. Smelters no longer need to be set up as close as possible to the source of fuel or iron ore. Indeed, both fuel and ore are now shipped by inexpensive water transportation from the far corners of the earth to fill the growing demands of such major steel-producing countries as the United States (Fig. 5-3) and Japan, where production of rich ores is not sufficient to meet requirements. A natural consequence of this trend has been a smaller need for possession of the high-grade iron resources requisite to the industrial growth of a country, as the industrial development of an iron-poor country such as Japan attests. It is apparent from Fig. 5-4 just how effective the modern transportation system has become. Only three of the major producers and consumers of pig iron fully meet their own needs for iron ore.

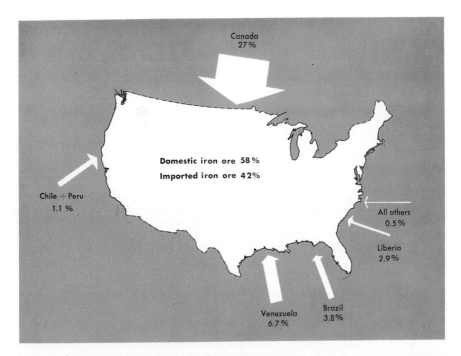

FIG. 5·3 Sources of iron ore used for production of iron and steel in the United States. The percentages are averages for the years 1978–1982. (After U.S. Bureau of Mines.)

FIG. 5-4 Comparison of the main smelters of pig iron (the main consumers) and the main suppliers of iron ore in 1981. With the exceptions of the U.S.S.R., Brazil, and Canada, none of the major smelters of pig iron today meet their own requirements for iron ore.

SMELTING OF PIG IRON (Millions of metric tons)		METAL CONTENT OF IRON ORE MINED (Millions of metric tons)	
USSR	106.3	USSR	133.1
Japan	80.0	Brazil	65.0
U.S.A.	66.9	Australia	54.6
China	34.0	U.S.A.	47.3
Federal Republic of Germany	31.9	China	35.1
France	17.0	Canada	31.9
Hungary	12.3	India	25.7
Poland	11.0	Republic of South Africa	18.1
Brazil	10.9	Sweden	15.1
Canada	9.9	Liberia	12.2
Czechoslovakia	9.9	Venezuela	9.6
Belgium	9.8	France	6.8
37 Other countries	100.9	42 Other countries	45.0
	500.8		499.5

Iron Resources

Iron forms four important ore minerals (Table A-2). The property of iron that most strongly affects its concentration in nature is its ability to exist in more than one oxidation state. At the surface of the earth, where oxygen is abundant, only the ferric or Fe^{+3} state is stable, and ferric iron minerals such as hematite and goethite occur. Beneath the surface, where free oxygen is absent, ferrous iron, Fe^{+2}, is stable, and ferrous minerals such as siderite, or mixed ferric-ferrous minerals such as magnetite, are found.

There are three important classes of iron deposits:

1. Deposits associated with igneous rocks
2. Residual deposits
3. Sedimentary deposits

When a magma begins to crystallize after upward intrusion into cooler portions of the crust, several mechanisms may lead to deposits associated with the resulting igneous rock. A magma is a complex liquid containing many compounds; it does not crystallize at a fixed temperature as simple liquids do, but instead it crystallizes over a temperature range, first one mineral forming, then another, until it is all solidified as an igneous rock containing several different minerals. If one or more of the minerals are denser than the parent magma, they may sink rapidly and form concentrations by *magmatic segregation* on the floor of the magma chamber. When the entire magma has crystallized to an igneous rock, the segregated layers of heavy minerals may prove to be rich ores. An interesting magmatic deposit occurs in the Bushveld Complex in South Africa. The Bushveld is a spectacularly layered series of igneous rocks resulting from magmatic segregation; a 2-meter–thick layer in the upper part of the complex is almost entirely magnetite. The magnetite in this case is not quite pure, but it is nevertheless valuable because it contains one percent vanadium, which is an important alloying element for certain steels.

Early-formed minerals in a cooling magma tend to be anhydrous and free of volatiles such as fluorine and chlorine. As crystallization continues, therefore, the residual liquid becomes increasingly enriched in, and even saturated with, volatile components. Eventually the volatiles start to escape and alter the rocks surrounding the magma chamber. *Contact metamorphic* deposits immediately adjacent to igneous rock are formed in this fashion. Finally, the escaping volatiles, which are commonly called *hydrothermal fluids* because they are hot and usually aqueous, may follow well-defined flow channels and, as they cool, deposit some of the dissolved matter that they carry and thus form *hydrothermal deposits*.

Iron deposits with igneous affiliations are of two kinds. The first are contact metamorphic, and they are usually small but very rich bodies of either hematite or magnetite. Only a few are large enough to be worked, although unusually large concentrations were once mined in Pennsylvania at Cornwall and are still mined in Utah at Iron Springs and at Mount Magnitaya in the Ural Mountains of the U.S.S.R. Because of their relatively small size, deposits with igneous affiliations do not hold much promise of great undiscovered riches; they may be locally important but are not likely to be major factors in the future of the world's iron resources. The second are hydrothermal in origin. When volcanism occurs beneath the sea, seawater enters the pile of hot rocks, becomes heated, and leaches iron compounds from the rocks. When the hot solution rises again to the seafloor, forming a submarine hot spring, iron oxide and silica are deposited on the seafloor. Such submarine, volcanic-associated iron deposits are known as Algoma-type iron ores. They have apparently been forming on earth since about 3.5 billion years ago to the present day. A few Algoma-type deposits, especially in Canada, are large enough and sufficiently rich to be worked, but most are too lean or too small to be of interest.

Residual deposits of iron minerals are formed wherever weathering occurs and the ferrous iron present in a rock is oxidized to form insoluble ferric minerals. This accounts for the brown, yellow, black, and red colors of weathered rocks, and also for many of the familiar soil colors. If the same weathering process removes more soluble minerals, the iron oxides and hydroxides remain concentrated as a residue. The process is known to have been active from Precambrian times to the present, and iron deposits formed in this way are very widespread. Commonly called brown ores, because of the color of their main mineral constituent, goethite, the residual deposits were among the first to be exploited. Individual deposits of rich residual ores are small, however, often containing only a few tens of thousands of tons, and do not lend themselves to the large-scale mechanized mining required by the modern iron industry. The importance of rich brown ores has therefore declined in recent time and will continue to do so for the immediate future. Where potential resources for the distant future are concerned, however, residual iron deposits are of considerable importance. In the tropics, where rainfall is high, soils tend to be extensively leached of soluble constituents but enriched in iron, because ferric iron compounds are essentially insoluble. These soils are called *laterites*. Lateritic soils are often too barren for concentrated agriculture, but they may contain up to 30 percent or more iron; although they are too low-grade to be worked today, laterites may eventually become a major source of iron. The tonnages available exceed those from all other sources by at least a factor of ten, but it should not be overlooked that because laterites are just a kind of soil, their mining would create massive environmental problems.

The sedimentary iron deposits account for most of the world's current production, as well as for reserves and potential resources for the foreseeable future. Though intensively studied for more than 100 years, some aspects of the origin of sedimentary iron deposits remain a mystery. There are no places where iron-rich sediments similar to those found in the geological record are known to be forming; the origin of the ancient deposits must therefore be deduced from many different lines of evidence. The lack of modern equivalents for the ancient iron-rich sediments once again emphasizes a point stressed earlier in the book: Mineral deposits are not growing second crops.

Sedimentary iron ores are *chemical sedimentary deposits,* which means that their constituents were transported in solution and deposited as chemical precipitates. This fact presents a great dilemma. The common iron mineral in sediments is either hematite or goethite, both of which are essentially insoluble in sea, lake, or river water because they are ferric iron compounds. But as we have seen, weathering at the earth's surface converts all the ferrous iron in a rock to the ferric state. How, then, could the iron have been transported in solution? The only way iron can readily be moved in the hydrosphere is to keep it in the more soluble ferrous state, which is impossible in surface waters today because of oxygen in the atmosphere, or else to somehow change the normally neutral or slightly alkaline surface waters into acid waters, in which ferric hydroxide is slightly more soluble. During the past 570 million years, which is the time from the beginning of the Cambrian to the present and is referred to as the Phanerozoic Eon, there have been a number of times when local circumstances occurred that led to ferrous iron being transported in solution below the surface. Because the solutions moved below the surface, they were shielded from oxygen in the atmosphere. When the subsurface solutions seeped upward, the iron was immediately oxidized and precipitated as goethite. The Phanerozoic iron deposits seem to have formed in restricted basins, lakes, or coastal embayments from less than a kilometer up to about 100 kilometers in diameter, and they clearly formed as a result of special and local, rather than worldwide, conditions. The special conditions, as far as we can decipher, were, first, a warm and humid climate which allowed a thick cover of deeply rooted plants to develop on the land surface, and second, soils and permeable rocks penetrated by ground waters rich in carbon dioxide from the subsurface production by root processes, and rich in organic acids from plant decay. The leached iron apparently moved out via subsurface routes to the sea. Where the debouching area was the open ocean, the iron was quickly dispersed, but in special cases where the debouching area was a shallow, restricted basin, the iron was trapped and accumulated as a chemical sediment. Because surface waters also run into the ocean and local basins, these deposits characteristically contain a lot of other mineral debris and fossils brought in by the surface waters.

Iron ores of the Phanerozoic type are important because they supply most of the iron ore mined in the United Kingdom, France, Germany, and Belgium, where, as a group, the ores are often called Minette-type. Similar ores, called the Clinton-type, have historically been mined in North America from Newfoundland to Birmingham, Alabama. The worldwide importance of the ore type is decreasing, however, because most of the North American mines are now closed, and the accessible parts of the European ores are being rapidly depleted. The ore that has taken the place of the Phanerozoic sedimentary iron deposits is one of the most remarkable rock types on earth—the so-called Lake Superior-type banded iron formations.

The period in the earth's history when the greatest amount of the iron-rich sediments were laid down, in Lake Superior-type deposits, extended from about 2.6 to 1.8 billion years ago. Lake Superior-type ores are named for the area in North America where they were first studied, but these ancient sediments are found on all continents, and we can only guess at how they formed. At first look, the Lake Superior-type ores resemble the Algoma-type because they consist of silica and iron oxide minerals. Close examination reveals that the Lake Superior-type ores formed in sedimentary basins and were apparently not closely associated with submarine volcanism. One condition that seems to have been needed to form the deposits was a long period of erosion and denudation of a continental mass, followed by a shallow inundation by the sea. The extensive erosion that preceded inundation left little detrital material to be carried in suspension; thus, slowly accumulating chemical precipitates were relatively more important in the new marine basin. One of the striking features of the Lake Superior-type ores is the paucity of detrital material. Although we have no direct proof, it is believed that at this early stage in the earth's history the atmosphere might have had a different composition. There was probably much less free oxygen, and the content of carbon dioxide was probably higher, perhaps as much as 10 to 100 times higher than it is at present. Under such conditions the surface waters would have been less oxidizing and slightly acid, allowing more iron to be moved in solution and eventually to be precipitated as iron oxide and hydroxide minerals in the shallow seas. The source of the iron is still somewhat of a mystery. Possibly it was leached from the land, but many scientists believe that the iron was added to seawater by submarine volcanism or that it was dissolved out of marine sediments.

Transportation of iron in surface waters is only one of the interesting problems associated with the Lake Superior-type iron ores. The sediments are laid down in repetitive bands of iron-rich and silica-rich layers—often in layers less than a millimeter thick. The banded texture is so striking that the rocks are commonly called *banded iron formations* [Fig. 5-5(A)]. The silica-rich layers are now cherts—exceedingly fine-grained quartz resulting from the recrystallization of colloidal silica. Fossil remains of primitive microscopic plants which were apparently growing in the shallow seas of the time [Fig. 5-5(B)] are sometimes preserved in such chert. These microscopic plants, first found in the Gunflint Formation but now identified in many banded iron formations around the world, are among the oldest fossils known, predating the abundant fossil record which began 570 million years ago by 2,000 million years. Whatever the circumstances were that caused the precipitation of banded iron formations, we are forced to conclude that they must not have been unusual, for the formations are found in many places around the world where rocks of

0 10 20 30 40 50 60 70 80 90 100
MILLIMETERS

A   B

FIG. 5-5 (A) Photograph of a specimen of banded iron formation from the Transvaal Basin, Rep. South Africa. The chert-rich bands (light) which alternate with the iron-rich bands (dark) are of uncertain origin: Some conclude an explosive growth of primitive microscopic organisms during the summer months, while others favor seasonal changes in the rate of evaporation. (B) Fragment of a primitive microscopic plant approximately two billion years old from the Gunflint Iron Formation, Ontario, magnified 2,000 times. (Courtesy E. Barghoorn and Tyler, *Science*, v. 147. Copyright 1965 by the American Association for the Advancement of Science.)

suitable age occur (Fig. 5-6); we must further conclude that conditions suitable for their formation have apparently not been present on the earth for at least 1.8 billion years.

The Lake Superior-type banded iron formations contain from 15 to 40 percent iron; this was traditionally considered too low to warrant recovery. Where the iron formations have been elevated and exposed at the surface, however, chemical weathering has often removed the associated siliceous or carbonate minerals and left an enriched residual ore containing 55 percent iron or more [Fig. 5-7(A) and (B)]. The great Precambrian iron deposits of the Lake Superior regions and the Laborador Trough in North America, of Cerro Bolivar in Venezuela and Minas Gerais in Brazil, of the Hamersley Range in Australia, of Krivoi Rog in the Ukraine, and in many other parts of the world are all extensive iron formations in which local zones have been enriched by the leaching of silica. Until 40 years ago the unleached and therefore unconcentrated iron formations below the rich ores had not been mined; after the depletion of the rich ore in the United States, ways were developed to mine and beneficiate the unleached ores—called *taconites*—in the Lake Superior district.

The mining of taconites is a good example of the manner in which tech-

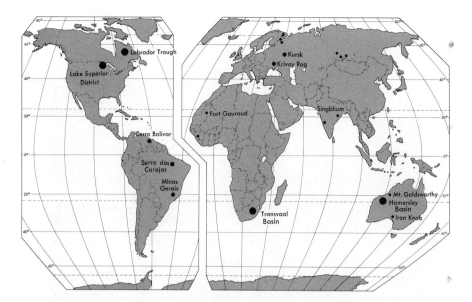

FIG. 5-6 Location of some major banded iron formations of the Lake Superior-type. These formations assure abundant iron resources far into the future.

nological advances can influence the value of potential resources. When first considered after World War II, taconites were considered to be expensive—even desperate—alternatives to the dwindling supplies of rich ores in the Lake Superior district. When production of the lean ores was begun, however, it was discovered that they could be beneficiated by using differences in the magnetism and density of the iron minerals and the admixed silica minerals. It was also found that (1) pellets formed from the concentrate made stronger and more efficient blast furnace feed than traditional ores, and (2) consequent savings in smelting and transportation more than offset the extra costs of mining and beneficiation. Taconite pellets have now become the standard of quality in the industry; by 1983 they accounted for more than 75 percent of U.S. production.

Reserves of leached and enriched iron ores are large—many billions of tons—but they are miniscule compared to the amount present in the unaltered iron formations. Estimates by the U.S. Geological Survey in 1965 showed that taconite reserves in the Lake Superior region alone exceeded 10^{11} tons of iron. Other estimates revealed that even larger potential resources—in the Transvaal, the Ukraine, the Hamersley Range of Western Australia, the Labrador Trough of northeastern Canada, and Minas Gerais in Brazil.

Considering that the world's present consumption of iron ore is less than 10^9 tons a year, the potential resources of iron are so greatly in excess of projected needs, even assuming liberal growth rates, that it seems safe to assert that many centuries will pass before depletion of present ores becomes a se-

A

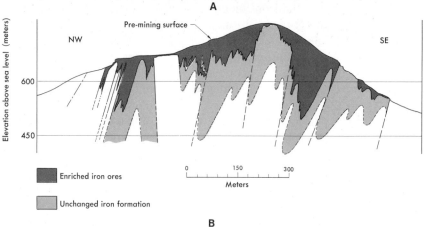

B

FIG. 5-7 (A) Aerial view of Cerro Bolivar, Venezuela, and the mining operations on its summit. The hard and resistant mass of banded iron formation stands above the surrounding plain as an erosion remnant. (Courtesy of Orinoco Mining Company.) (B) A cross section through Cerro Bolivar, showing the rich iron ores formed by secondary enrichment of the original iron formation. (After J. C. Ruckmick, 1963, *Economic Geology*, v. 58, p. 222.)

rious problem. Mr. Carnegie's perceptive remarks, quoted at the beginning of the chapter, were right on target; when thought was given to the future, a way was developed by which the lean ores replaced the rich. As will become apparent in the next section, Mr. Carnegie's remarks could now be applied to bauxite, the common ore of aluminum.

ALUMINUM

Aluminum is even more abundant in the earth's crust than iron is, and, because of its lightness, metallic aluminum has a more desirable weight/ strength ratio than iron does. The element was first separated in a pure form in 1827. It is very difficult to smelt. For a while the metal was so rare and so valuable that it was the fashion among French royalty to use aluminum knives and forks! By the end of the nineteenth century and the early part of the twentieth, industrial methods for producing aluminum metal of high purity had been developed. From that time on, the production and number of uses of aluminum have steadily increased. The world's production of aluminum exceeded 15 million metric tons in 1981. Production dropped to about 13 million metric tons in 1982 due to the worldwide economic recession, but it is expected to exceed 20 million metric tons within a few years. Aluminum has, in addition to its desirable strength and weight properties, a high resistance to corrosion, and it is a good conductor of electricity. Most of the technological uses take advantage of one or more of these properties; as a result, aluminum has challenged iron for some of its structural purposes and copper for some of its electrical uses; it is estimated, for example, that 90 percent of the new electrical transmission lines in the United States contain aluminum conductors. Aluminum also has its own distinctive properties, and has proved to be a highly versatile metal for applications in the construction, transportation, and packaging industries.

The smelting of aluminum requires large expenditures of electrical power; each ton of aluminum requires energy equivalent to that produced from the burning of 7 tons of coal. The aluminum industry consumes approximately 3 percent of the electric power generated in the United States. As aluminum production grows, it becomes increasingly desirable to ship aluminum ores to sources of inexpensive electrical power, such as the hydroelectric plants built along the Columbia River in the Pacific Northwest and in the sparsely populated regions of northern Canada. High power consumption has been the most important feature in determining the distribution of aluminum producers around the world.

Aluminum Resources

Aluminum, like iron, is found in many minerals. So far, however, almost all aluminum has been produced from three aluminum hydroxide minerals: gibbsite, boehmite, and diaspore. This use pattern introduces a curious anomaly. Aluminum is the third most abundant element in the crust, but its hydroxide compounds are among the rarer minerals. As a consequence, the reserves and potential resources of traditional aluminum ores are severely limited; they are also severely geographically restricted.

Minerals formed by igneous processes and by metamorphism are stable deep in the earth's crust, an environment in which large bodies of free water do not exist; such minerals are often anhydrous, or at best contain very little water. When brought to the surface, they are no longer stable; although the rate of chemical change to a more stable form is slow, they are gradually transformed into new minerals, most of which are hydrous. This transformation at the earth's surface is called *chemical weathering*. During chemical weathering, elements such as Na, K, Ca, and Mg are constitutents of relatively soluble compounds and are soon removed. The residue is a lateritic capping (Fig. 5-8). Most laterites are iron-rich, but some are aluminum-rich, because they contain the aluminum hydroxide minerals, and are called *bauxites* (after the little village of Les Baux in southern France, where they were first recognized in 1821).

Bauxites apparently form only under special conditions of tropical weathering. On a low-lying or relatively flat surface, rainwater runoff is slow, and mechanical removal of weathering products in suspension is minimal. Even though the solubility of most minerals is extremely low, the most effective way of moving material in low-lying areas is in solution. The high rainfall and warm climates of tropical areas speed the process greatly.

In addition to rainfall, topography, and temperature, the acidity of the leaching waters is important in the formation of bauxites. After the removal of most elements, a residue rich in clays, such as kaolinite ($Al_2Si_2O_5(OH)_4$) remains. Kaolinite, too, will dissolve. If the water percolating down is very acid, the mineral goes into solution completely; if the water is very slightly acid, only the silica component of the kaolinite is removed in solution, and aluminum hydroxide minerals are precipitated and left behind as bauxite. The process is slow and involves repeated solution and deposition. As a result, bauxites commonly have a distinctive *pisolitic* texture (Fig. 5-9).

FIG. 5-8 Leaching of the most soluble components during chemical weathering leaves a lateritic capping in which the less soluble aluminum and iron hydroxides are concentrated. When aluminum hydroxides predominate, the laterite is called a bauxite.

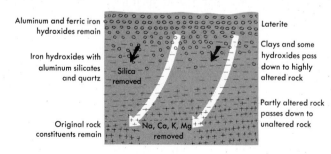

FIG. 5-9 Pisolitic texture of
bauxite from Arkansas
develops through repeated
solution and deposition. Each
pisolite is about 1–2 centimeters in diameter and consists of a great many fine
layers of aluminum hydroxide
minerals. (B. J. Skinner)

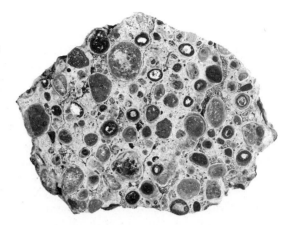

The source rocks for bauxites have a wide range of compositions. Some source rocks do not contain much aluminum to begin with, but most tend to have relatively low silica contents compared with other rocks. In fact, several of the world's largest bauxite deposits are developed on limestones; these consist largely of calcium carbonate, but they usually contain small amounts of clays and even smaller amounts of iron minerals, so that the laterites formed from them are bauxitic. In a tropical climate, limestone dissolves rapidly and the clay residues remain; the acidity of the waters leaching the limestone is apparently just right for the development of bauxite.

Bauxites are widespread in the world but are concentrated in the tropics. Even where they are found in presently temperate conditions such as southern France and Arkansas, it is clear that the climate was tropical when they formed. Because bauxites are superficial deposits, they are exposed and vulnerable to mechanical weathering processes. Bauxites are unknown in glaciated regions, for example, because the overriding glaciers scrape all the soft materials off the surface. Because of their vulnerability to later erosion processes, most bauxites are geologically young: More than 90 percent of them formed during the past 60 million years and the largest of all formed in the tropics during the last 25 million years.

Tropical regions are among the least developed parts of the world, and it is only since World War II that they have been extensively explored for bauxites. The results have been particularly successful; vast reserves of rich ores have been discovered in the tropical regions of Australia, the Caribbean, Africa, and South America.

In 1967 the world's bauxite resources were estimated by the U.S. Geological Survey to consist of 5.8×10^9 metric tons of reserves and 9.6×10^9 metric tons of potential resources that were either too lean or too remotely situated to be called reserves at that time. Approximately 73 percent of the total reserves plus resources were in the tropical regions of northern Queensland in Australia, Guinea and Cameroon in Africa, Surinam and Guyana in

South America, and in Jamaica. The remainder were widely dispersed, with the larger portions in Asia and Europe. Since 1967 new deposits have been found in many places, especially in Brazil, the countries of west Africa, Taiwan, and Indonesia. Some of the potential resources of 1967 have become reserves as engineers have learned to process poorer materials and as transportation has improved. The same scientist who was responsible for the 1967 estimate suggested that discovered bauxite resources in 1974 were 20×10^9 metric tons, of which at least 10×10^9 metric tons were reserves. By the end of 1982 the figures had increased again, though not so dramatically, as a result of new discoveries. The total bauxite resources have not been estimated very carefully, but the 1982 figure was about 25×10^9 metric tons. The figure may increase still further, but the likelihood seems high that the discovery days for giant bauxite deposits are over because most of the tropical land areas have now been explored. The restricted conditions under which bauxite forms make it unlikely that resources will rise by factors of ten, so the present estimate of 25×10^9 metric tons is probably realistic.

The total, 25×10^9 metric tons, sounds very large, but it is actually tiny compared to the huge resources of iron ore, for which individual deposits far exceed the entire inventory of bauxite resources. When we consider that even a rich bauxite will only yield about a third of its weight in aluminum, and that production of new aluminum is expected to exceed 20×10^6 metric tons a year in the near future, concern expressed for the long-term adequacy of bauxite resources is well-founded. Bauxite reserves are like oil reserves—they are adequate for the immediate future and reliable through the end of the present century and the early decades of the next, but they will not be capable of sustaining our use patterns far into the future.

Although resources of bauxite are adequate to last into the next century, economic and political factors make the development of aluminum from other sources seem inevitable. Aluminum-consuming countries are not large bauxite producers (Table 5-1), so one factor is simply the rising cost of bauxite as the producing countries demand larger returns from the importing countries by increasing costs for land and mining rights, by raising taxes, and by requiring large capital investments to provide jobs and to bolster local economies. Other factors include rising costs of transportation, plant, and mining facilities, threats of nationalization before investments are returned and profits secured, and the stability of governments. Financial pressures are so strong that many experts suspect that some of today's reserves will again slip back to become potential resources.

There are, therefore, two pressures facing bauxite: One we might call a sociopolitical pressure, the other a pressure of low abundance. Both lead to the same conclusions—alternative sources will be developed to replace bauxite. If bauxite won't serve for the future, what alternatives are there? The possible candidates for alternate supply sources are confined to the material listed in Table 5-1. Aluminum has already been extracted from the silicate mineral nepheline in the U.S.S.R., and from the sulfate alunite in Japan, the U.S.S.R.,

Table 5-1 Principal bauxite-mining and aluminum-smelting countries, 1981.

BAUXITE MINING	(millions of metric tons)	ALUMINUM SMELTING	(millions of metric tons)
Australia	25.5	U.S.A.	4.5
Guinea	12.1	U.S.S.R.*	1.8
Jamaica	11.7	Canada	1.2
Brazil	5.3	Japan	0.8
U.S.S.R.	4.6	Fed. Rep. Germany	0.7
Surinam	3.7	Norway	0.6
Greece	3.3	France	0.4
Yugoslavia	3.2	35 other countries	5.1
16 other countries	16.2		

*produced in part from nonbauxite ore
(*After U.S. Bureau of Mines*).

Mexico, and in the United States on a test basis. Unfortunately, however, both nepheline and alunite suffer the same problems of geographic restriction and overall abundance that plague bauxite. Much more hopeful are the possibilities of producing aluminum from more common minerals.

Clays, such as kaolinite, are formed during the weathering cycle of most rocks and, following quartz, are the most abundant minerals in newly deposited sediments. If production costs could be lowered, clays could be used right now; successful test plants have already been operated in the United States, the U.S.S.R., and Poland, but the costs are considerably greater than those for producing aluminum from bauxite. This is so because kaolinite is a silicate mineral, so even more energy is needed in the reduction process. If the necessary technical and economic steps could be taken, aluminum could be freed from resource supply problems. All countries have clays in abundance, and the potential resources dwarf those of iron.

Aluminum from clay is only one of several possibilities. Referring to Table 5-2, we see that other opportunities exist. The aluminum silicate minerals, andalusite, sillimanite, and kyanite, form by metamorphism of clay-rich sedimentary rocks. Like their parent materials they are abundant and widespread, but they must be beneficiated before processing. A plant to produce aluminum from the aluminum silicates has been built in southern France.

The most abundant family of minerals in earth's crust is the feldspar family, of which there are three chemical variants: $KAlSi_3O_8$, $NaAlSi_3O_8$, and $CaAl_2Si_2O_8$. The calcium feldspar anorthite contains about 19 percent aluminum by weight and is the main constituent of a rock called anorthosite. Test plants in the U.S.A. and Norway have shown that production of aluminum from anorthosite is possible. Abundance of anorthosite is hardly a limitation. To a depth of 30 meters in the Laramie Range, Wyoming, anorthosite deposits

Table 5·2 Current and potentially important ore minerals of aluminum*

PRESENT-DAY ORES

Mineral	Composition	Content of Al (percent)	Remarks
BOEHMITE, DIASPORE	$HAlO_2$	45	Principal constituents of bauxite
GIBBSITE	H_3AlO_3	34.6	

ORES FOR THE FUTURE

Mineral	Composition	Content of Al (percent)	Remarks
ANDALUSITE, KYANITE SILLIMANITE	Al_2SiO_5	33.5	Used by Sweden during World War II
KAOLINITE (the most aluminous clay; any clay-rich sediment can be used)	$Al_2Si_2O_5(OH)_4$	20.9	Successful test plants by the U.S.A., the U.S.S.R., Poland. Used by Japan and Germany during World War II
ANORTHOSITE (calcium feldspar is an abundant constituent)	$CaAl_2Si_2O_8$	19.4	Successful test plants in the U.S.A. and Norway.

(Continued)

contain an estimated 30×10^9 metric tons, and for the United States as a whole, the figure is in excess of 10^{11} metric tons. Research and test production of aluminum from anorthosite is proceeding, and some authorities believe that it is a more likely successor to bauxite than are the clay minerals.

The remaining alternate sources in Table 5-2 offer fewer technological problems than clays or anorthosite but, like alunite and nepheline, seem to suffer from supply restrictions. Perhaps the most realistic assessment of aluminum is that it is a commodity with vast potential resources waiting for some innovative technological advances, but that production of aluminum will always be energy-intensive and expensive.

MANGANESE

Manganese is essential as an additive for steels to combat the weakening effects of small amounts of oxygen and sulfur. Up to 7 kilograms of man-

Table 5-2 (*cont.*)

ORES FOR THE FUTURE

Mineral	Composition	Content of Al (percent)	Remarks
NEPHELINE	$NaAlSiO_4$	18.4	Successfully tested by U.S.A. and Japan. Used on limited scale in the U.S.S.R.
ALUNITE	$K_2Al_6(OH)_{12}(SO_4)_4$	19.6	Successfully tested in the U.S.A. and Japan. Used for limited production in the U.S.S.R.
DAWSONITE	$NaAl(OH)_2CO_3$	18.7	Can possibly be produced as a by-product of oil shale production in the U.S.A.
WAVELLITE (one of several similar minerals that occur together)	$Al_3(PO_4)_2(OH)_3 \cdot 5H_2O$	19.6	A by-product from phosphate mining. Now wasted.

*Further discussion of potential materials may be found in Bulletin 1228 (1967) and Professional Paper 820 (1973), both published by the U.S. Geological Survey.

ganese are required for every ton of steel produced, and no satisfactory substitute has been found.

Manganese, like iron, has more than one oxidation state, and its distribution is controlled in large part by this property. Manganese is readily concentrated by chemical sedimentary processes; in fact all of the important manganese resources of the world are in sedimentary rocks, combined sedimentary and volcanic rocks, or in residual deposits formed by the leaching of primary deposits. As is the case with iron, the most oxidized compounds of manganese are the least soluble and are those concentrated in both residual and sedimentary deposits.

The world's largest reserves, in which pyrolusite (MnO_2) and other manganese minerals occur in chemical sedimentary deposits very similar to Phanerozoic iron deposits, are found in the U.S.S.R., at Chiaturi in Georgia, and at Nikopol in the Ukraine. These two deposits contain reserves of hundreds of millions of tons and account for more than 75 percent of the world's rich manganese ores. Important residual deposits, mainly of pyrolusite and psilomelane ($Mn_2O_3 \cdot 2H_2O$), are found in South Africa, India, Australia, Brazil, Gabon, and China. Like bauxite, the rich residual deposits of manganese oxides are concentrated in the tropics where high rainfall and deep weathering are common. Though widely distributed, the world's reserve of manganese in ores amenable to mining was estimated by the U.S. Bureau of Mines in 1970 to be only about 25×10^9 metric tons. Compared to the 1981 world production of above 25×10^6 metric tons of manganese ore, this is not a large figure (Table 5-3). It is possible that further exploration in tropical regions will uncover large sources of rich manganese ores, but it is likely that we will soon have to turn to new and unconventional sources.

One of the largest potential resources of manganese, and one that has excited discussion and speculation for many years, rests on the ocean floors. During the years from 1873 to 1876, the Royal Society of London sent the ship *Challenger* on an epoch-making voyage around the world to gather data on the waters, animals, plants, and bottom deposits of the oceans. One of the most interesting discoveries was of an abundance of black nodules, as long as several centimeters in diameter, on the floors of the three major oceans (Fig. 5-10). The nodules are mixtures of manganese and iron oxides and hydroxides. Although popularly called manganese nodules, a more correct term is ferromanganese nodules. Although the nodules have been intensively studied in recent years, some details of their origin remain puzzling. The manganese is probably derived in part from normal erosive processes on land and in part from the leaching of manganese by seawater from hot volcanic rocks extruded along the midocean ridges. Through a complex series of steps the manganese slowly migrates and accumulates in the deeper parts of the ocean.

The rate at which the nodules grow appears to be extremely slow—less than a millimeter per 1,000 years. They are widely spread on the seafloor, however, and it has been estimated that approximately 2×10^{12} metric tons

Table 5-3 Principal producers of manganese ore, 1981. The major consumers are the large iron- and steel-producing countries (Fig. 5-4).

	(Millions of Metric Tons)
U.S.S.R.	9.40
Rep. So. Africa	5.04
Brazil	1.90
China	1.60
India	1.50
Gabon	1.49
Australia	1.41

(After U.S. Bureau of Mines).

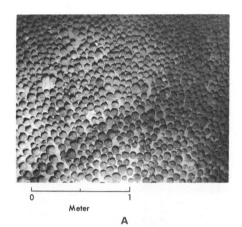

0   1
Meter

A

FIG. 5-10 (A) Photograph of the Pacific Ocean floor, 5,320 meters deep, showing a field of ferromanganese nodules. (Courtesy of Lamont-Doherty Geophysical Observatory of Columbia University.) (B) A ferromanganese nodule sliced in half to reveal the fine banding that results from the slow processes of chemical precipitation that form the nodules on the seafloor. The nodule is 10 centimeters long. (B. J. Skinner)

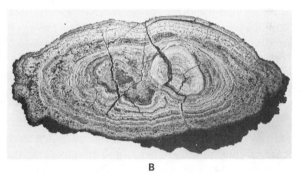

B

of nodules could be dredged from the bottom of the Pacific Ocean alone. These would yield 4×10^{11} metric tons of manganese.

Manganese nodules have already been dredged from the floor of the Pacific on a trial basis for commercial production by both Japanese and United States companies. It is not known when regular production may commence; curiously, though, when production does commence, it will probably not be for the manganese content, which may be no more than 25 percent, but instead for other metals. Nodules in certain areas contain several percent of copper, nickel, cobalt, and other scarce metals, and if separation techniques are successful, the first nodules will probably be produced to recover these metals. Manganese, if recovered at all, will be a by-product. What bottom dredging of the ocean might do to the seafloor remains an open question. Who will have the right to recover the material is also very much an open question and one that has been discussed at great length in the halls of the United Nations under the topic "Law of the Sea." When the ownership question is resolved, the question of how mining is to be monitored and policed is another vast problem for the future. An entire new field of legal expertise is already developing.

TITANIUM

The metal titanium, like aluminum, combines light weight with high strength and high resistance to corrosion. For some purposes—in the development of supersonic aircraft, for example—it has answered many technological needs. It is a difficult metal to work, however, and very energy-intensive to recover from its ores. Indeed, commercial production of titanium began only after World War II, and U.S. consumption had only reached 29,000 metric tons by 1981. It is still too early in the history of titanium to accurately estimate its ultimate importance to mankind, but its potential seems great.

By far the largest use of titanium, accounting for more than 90 percent of world consumption, is as the oxide (TiO_2), which is widely used as a white pigment for paints.

Ilmenite ($FeTiO_3$), the main ore mineral, is concentrated by magmatic segregation and is often found associated with anorthosites. The largest known titanium deposits in the world, at Allard Lake, Quebec, are of this kind, as are the deposits at Sanford Lake in the Adirondack Mountains of upper New York State, and at Blaafjeldite in Norway.

A second titanium mineral, rutile (TiO_2), is as common in the crust as ilmenite is, but there are no igneous, metamorphic, or hydrothermal processes by which large masses have become concentrated. There is, however, an entirely different way by which both rutile and ilmenite become concentrated. Both minerals are widely distributed in small amounts in igneous and metamorphic rocks; both are heavy and extremely resistant to attack from chemical weathering. Resistance to breakdown means that they are among the last minerals to disappear in the weathering cycle; when clays and other fine-grained breakdown products are carried away in suspension, the heavy, chemically resistant minerals remain behind and become concentrated in *placers* (see Chapter 6). Important placer deposits are worked in Australia, Sri Lanka (formerly Ceylon), India, Sierra Leone, the Republic of South Africa, and the U.S.S.R. Large reserves exist, and even larger potential resources are known; detrital ilmenite and rutile deposits on the Atlantic coastal shelf of the United States, for example, exceed 10^9 metric tons. Reserves and potential resources of the titanium minerals seem more than adequate for the far future.

MAGNESIUM

Magnesium is the lightest abundant and stable metal and, being strong, is in demand for the production of light corrosion-resistant alloys, especially alloys of magnesium and aluminum. The annual production of magnesium as a metal, however, is small compared to that of iron and aluminum—about 300,000 metric tons for the world in 1981. The main use of magnesium is not as a metal but in compounds, particularly the oxide (MgO), which has desirable thermal and electrical insulating properties. The major sources of magnesium are the sea, which contains an inexhaustible supply of the element (see Chapter 2), and the minerals dolomite, $CaMg(CO_3)_2$, and magnesite, $MgCO_3$, both of which are widespread in the crust. Dolomite occurs in marine sedimentary rocks and commonly forms an essential constituent of a rock called *dolostone*. Magnesite is found in sediments, residual concentrations, and hydrothermal deposits.

Reserves of magnesium are almost limitless and are so widely available to all nations that any discussion of their magnitude has little point. The only limits and constraints on our use of magnesium will be the inventiveness of our technology.

ABUNDANT METALS IN THE FUTURE

From the foregoing discussion it seems apparent that geochemical abundance in the earth's crust carries with it an assurance of resource abundance. Use of the abundant metals will not be limited by supplies of ores, but there probably are difficulties ahead as new kinds of ore minerals are used and as lower-grade ores must be processed. With the exception of aluminum, none of the challenges seems likely to produce major problems for present economic structures. Even for aluminum, solutions to technological problems will be found and will probably prevent challenges to societal use patterns of the metal. The geochemically scarce metals, to be discussed in the next chapter, lead to a very different set of conclusions.

six

the scarce metals

The foreseeable exhaustion of ores of some metals and the continually decreasing grade of most ore deposits now used warn that ample lead time will be needed for technology to work out such answers as it can and, similarly, to allow the economy and population density to make the necessary adjustments to changing mineral supplies. (T. S. Lovering, "Mineral Resources from the Land," in Resources and Man, *edited by P. Cloud, 1969, U.S. National Academy of Sciences.)*

The geochemically scarce metals are defined as those with crustal abundances below 0.1 percent. It is perhaps surprising to find that such common commodities as copper, lead, zinc, and nickel, all of which have large and growing rates of production (Fig. 6-1), are geochemically rare and belong in the scarce category along with gold, silver, and platinum. Most experts believe that it is in this group of metals that shortages are likely to develop first and that these are apt to pose a serious challenge to technological development. Indeed, some shortages are already upon us. Silver and gold production no longer meets present demands, and stockpiles and savings from past mining are being drawn upon.

The scarce metals are a vital group that speeded the development of the technological marvels of the last hundred years, such as the generation and distribution of electricity; telegraphic, radio, and television communication; aeronautics; rocketry; and nuclear power. The electrical industry, for example, would certainly have progressed more slowly without abundant and inexpensive supplies of copper. The threat for the future posed by shortages of scarce metals is that these same technological marvels, and others to come, may be imperiled. Unlimited supplies of uranium, for example, will be of little use if the essential metals required to construct nuclear power plants and to transmit and use the electricity so generated are not available.

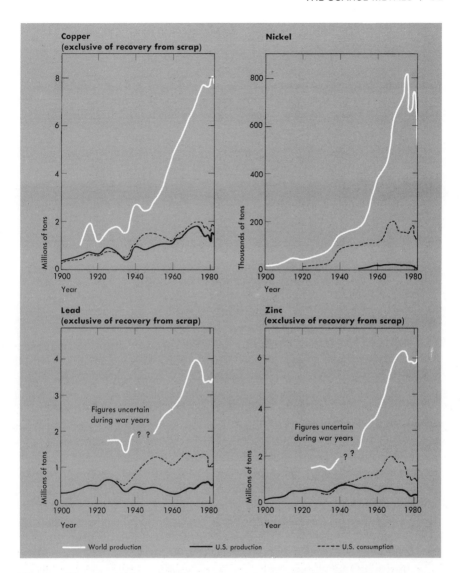

FIG. 6-1 World and U.S. production of several geochemically scarce metals, together with the U.S. consumption rate. The percentage consumed by the U.S. is steadily declining as the living standard of other countries increases. (After U.S. Bureau of Mines.)

The relative abundance of scarce metals in the crust is low, but the total amounts are large simply because the crust itself is large. It makes little sense to consider "average" rock as a potential source of scarce metal, although some have endorsed the idea; the huge tonnages that would have to be processed and the tremendous energy consumption needed to conduct the operation would defeat the project. Just how unprofitable the process would be is

Table 6-1 Calculated value of scarce metals in a metric ton of average granite.

Element	Concentration in average granite* (percent)	Price of metal (1982); $U.S./kg	Value of metal in a metric ton of granite; $U.S.
Thorium	0.002	$176	$3.52
Beryllium	0.0002	531	1.59
Lithium	0.003	44	1.32
Niobium	0.002	66	1.32
Tantalum	0.0002	132	0.30
Uranium	0.0005	25	0.12
Tungsten	0.0002	31	0.06
Gold	0.000002	14789	0.06
Zinc	0.005	0.99	0.05
Lead	0.0039	0.79	0.03
Molybdenum	0.0001	20	0.02
Copper	0.0024	1.83	0.02
Silver	0.0000036	338	0.01

*After Wedepohl (1978)

evident from Table 6-1, where the dollar values of scarce metals in an average granite are listed. If all could be recovered with a 100 percent yield, the total value of the scarce metals would only be $8.42, based on the prices of the metals at the end of 1982. Mining and crushing granite would cost about $8.50 a metric ton, and smelting the rock to recover the metals would probably cost many hundreds of dollars, so the proposition is obviously a poor one from an economic viewpoint. There is another obvious reason that processing common rock for scarce metals does not make much sense. If we were to process a granite it would surely be sensible to recover all metals present—abundant as well as scarce. This would lead to an oversupply of iron, aluminum, and other abundant metals, and an insufficient supply of scarce metals such as tin, silver, and copper. The reason is obvious: We do not use metals in proportion to their natural abundances. We consume scarce metals at a proportionally faster rate than we consume abundant metals.

Instead of attempting to win metals from *common* rocks, we have always sought *ore deposits,* the localized geological circumstances in which certain minerals, called ore minerals (Table A-2), carry high contents of desired metals and are sufficiently concentrated so that the metals can be won cheaply and rapidly. There is no reason to believe that the pattern will change in the future. A number of factors determine whether or not a local concentration can be considered an ore deposit. The present minimum concentrations are high (Fig. 6-2), even when all factors are favorable, although the minimums tend to change somewhat as mining becomes more efficient and prices change. We do not yet know how low the necessary concentration factors can be pushed be-

FIG. 6-2 The crustal abundances of geochemically scarce metals are so low that large concentrations above background average are needed before deposits can be profitably mined. The abundant metals require lower concentration factors to produce rich ores. The bracketed percentages are the minimum metal contents an ore must have before it can be mined under the most favorable circumstances with present day technology. Note that as the price of a metal goes up or down, its position will move on the diagram. Between 1969 and 1982, for example, the concentration factor needed for a viable gold deposit dropped from about 4,000 to 1,600, largely as a result of the rising price of gold.

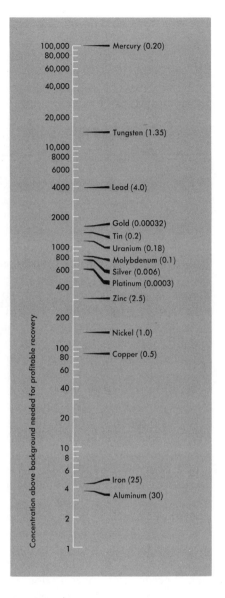

fore the cost of recovering the metals is so high that we must do without, or before substitutes such as cements, ceramics, plastics, or even abundant metals take their place. Technology too is a resource—of man's own ingenuity—and can be vitally important in developing potential resources of scarce metals. What is considered hopelessly impractical for exploitation by today's standards, or even by those projected for tomorrow, may well be tapped in the future because of technological advances.

DISTRIBUTION OF THE SCARCE METALS

The scarce metals are widely distributed, but, unlike the abundant metals, they rarely form separate minerals in common rocks. Instead, they reside in the structures of common rock-forming minerals, usually the silicates, with an atom of a scarce metal substituting for an atom of an abundant element. For example, nickel atoms can substitute for magnesium atoms in olivine (Mg_2SiO_4), although they usually do so only to the extent of a few hundred nickel atoms for every million atoms of magnesium, and lead atoms tend to substitute for potassium in feldspars. Substitution of foreign atoms causes strains in a mineral structure, and, accordingly, there are limits to the process; these are determined by temperature, pressure, and various chemical parameters related to the rock composition. In most common rocks and minerals, the limits are not exceeded and the scarce metals remain atomically locked in the host structures. To recover the scarce metals, the host mineral itself must be broken down, and this is an expensive chemical process because most silicate minerals are highly refractory and difficult to smelt. When the limits of atomic substitution are exceeded, however, substituting elements form separate minerals—for example, galena (PbS) in the case of lead; the way is then open for an inexpensive beneficiation process. The physical properties of galena differ markedly from those of the associated silicate minerals, and simple crushing, followed by concentration (based, for example, on density or surface property [flotation] differences) will produce an inexpensive, lead-rich concentrate of galena before the expensive chemical reduction process is started. The presence of a scarce metal in a separate mineral that has distinctly different physical properties from the associated nonore minerals has always been an important factor in the utilization of metals and the exploitation of their ores. It is significant, for example, that the scarce metal gallium, with a crustal abundance approximately twice that of lead, occurs almost exclusively as an element substituting in aluminum minerals and has never been of vital importance in technology. Had inexpensive sources of easily reduced gallium minerals been available, we would probably have many uses for gallium.

A graphic presentation of the differences between scarce metals locked in silicates by atomic substitution and scarce metals forming separate minerals is shown in Fig. 6-3. The lower line on the diagram shows the amount of energy needed to recover a kilogram of copper metal from a rock containing chalcopyrite ($CuFeS_2$) in a matrix of valueless silicate minerals. The line slopes upward toward low grades because more rock must be mined, crushed, and beneficiated to produce a given amount of chalcopyrite concentrate; more rocks mined means more energy used. But energy to smelt a given amount of chalcopyrite is always the same regardless of the grade of the ore from which it is obtained. The upper curve, which is a high energy curve, demonstrates the amount of energy that would be needed to get copper from a rock in which

FIG. 6-3 Energy used to extract metallic copper from ores containing sulfide minerals and from solid solution in silicate minerals of common rocks. The two curves are parallel but do not over-lap. The gap represents a mineralogical barrier to the trend to mine increasingly lower grade ores. All geochemically scarce metals seem to display this relationship.

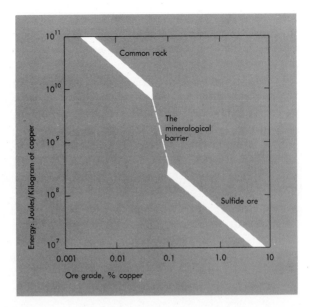

all the copper is present in atomic substitution in a common silicate mineral—the example is calculated for a mica called biotite, by making the assumption that 30 percent of the parent rock is biotite. The two lines are parallel, because the processes of mining, crushing, and beneficiating to produce a biotite concentrate are essentially the same as they are to produce a chalcopyrite concentrate. The difference between the lines is the energy requirement for smelting. Notice, however, that the sulfide mineral plot stops at a grade of about 0.1 percent Cu. Below a grade of about 0.1 percent, all copper is present as an atomic substitute. An exact grade cannot be stated because it will vary from one rock type to another. Similarly, the silicate curve only comes down to about 0.05 percent because we do not find common rocks that contain copper in silicates at high grades. This means that if we were ever to reach the point at which all sulfide ores had been mined out, including even the lowest-grade ores down to 0.1 percent, we would face a *mineralogical barrier.* Ores with grades below 0.1 percent would not only contain less copper, but the copper would also be much more difficult to recover because it would have to be released from its sites of atomic substitution in silicate mineral. A vital question is, therefore, what fraction of the copper in earth's crust is present in ore minerals and what fraction in atomic substitution?

Unfortunately, a very large fraction of the scarce metals in the crust—more than 99.9 percent and probably as much as 99.99 percent—occurs as atomic substitutes in silicate minerals. The 0.1 percent or less is the tiny fraction present in ore minerals that can be beneficiated. Fortunately the ore minerals tend to occur in small, concentrated volumes of rock—ore deposits—so it is feasible to believe that we may ultimately find and mine most of the ore minerals in the crust.

Atomic substitution can occur in all kinds of minerals, not just silicates. Under some circumstances atomic substitution can actually be helpful. Elements such as silver and cadmium—which, because of low abundance levels, rarely form separate minerals and even less commonly form ore deposits—are produced largely as by-products from the ore minerals of copper, lead, and zinc in which they are carried by atomic substitution. Silver, for example, commonly substitutes for copper in the ore minerals tetrahedrite ($Cu_{12}Sb_4S_{13}$) and chalcocite (Cu_2S), and it substitutes for lead in the mineral galena (PbS). Recovery of silver as a by-product is now so large that in 1982, of the 25 largest silver producers in the United States, 15 were primarily lead, zinc, and copper producers, whereas only 10 mined their ores primarily for their silver content. The difference between recovering metals from atomic substitution in sulfides and silicates is that sulfides are easily smelted while silicates are not.

Ore Deposits of Scarce Metals

An ore deposit is a mineral deposit from which one or more materials can be extracted profitably. Two essential features of ore deposits have already been discussed: Ore deposits are localized volumes within which certain chemical elements are concentrated far above the crustal average; they are places where special minerals are found. Oil pools, coal fields, and enriched cappings over banded iron formations are examples of ores, but the scarce metals present special problems of their own that deserve separate mention.

Scarce metal ore deposits tend either to have sharply defined boundaries, such as the walls of veins, or to have gradational boundaries, as in some copper deposits, that grade into average rock over distances of tens, or at most a few hundreds, of meters. Many deposits are rather like raisins in a fruitcake. They also tend to be small compared to deposits of abundant metals. For example, large copper deposits contain between 10^6 and 10^7 metric tons of copper; the largest known copper deposit does not contain more than 5×10^7 metric tons of the metal. Many iron deposits, on the other hand, exceed 10^9 metric tons. The maximum size of scarce metal deposits and the number of large deposits of a given metal are both apparently related to their crustal abundance [Fig. 6-4(A) and (B)]. The reasons for these relationships have not been completely explained, but they are clearly related to the degree of concentration needed for the deposit of a scarce metal to be minable ore. The scarcer the metal in the crust, the greater the needed concentration and the less likely it is for all the special concentrating factors to be working at the same time and place.

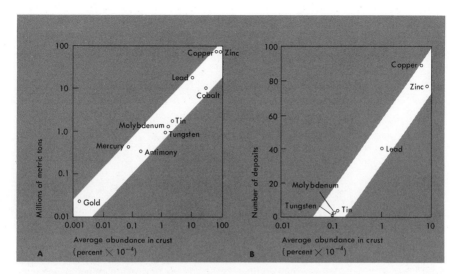

FIG. 6-4 (A) The largest known ore deposit for each scarce metal is approximately proportional to its crustal abundance. (B) The lower the concentration factor and the higher the crustal abundance, the more common it is for large ore deposits to form. The number of deposits containing a million metric tons or more of a scarce metal is proportional to the crustal abundance. Note that logarithmic axes are used for both graphs.

Discovery of Scarce Metal Deposits

As new lands have been explored and prospected, they have followed patterns similar to those shown in Fig. 6-5. The number of ore deposits discovered, and therefore the number of working mines (curve A), climbs rapidly due to an initial phase of prospecting. After a time, however, as smaller mines are worked out, the rate of discovery no longer exceeds the rate of depletion and closing. The number of working mines then declines and eventually must reach zero (although no large country has quite reached this point so far). During the active working life of the mines, the production of metal increases (curve B), although the production must lag behind the mine curve because mines must be discovered before they can be worked. The metal production curve must also eventually decline to zero when the last mine closes. In industrial countries in which mineral output is largely used for internal consumption, the increasing demands soon make it difficult for internal production to satisfy needs. Importation commences (curve C) and as time passes a growing amount of the metals consumed come in from lands abroad.

The curves in Fig. 6-5 are supported by recent history. Three prominent industrial countries are plotted in their relative positions. As Europeans expanded into and explored the Americas, Africa, Asia, and Australia, they found a great many ore deposits. At a much earlier time they had been successful in Europe, too, but, as was pointed out by R. J. Forbes some years

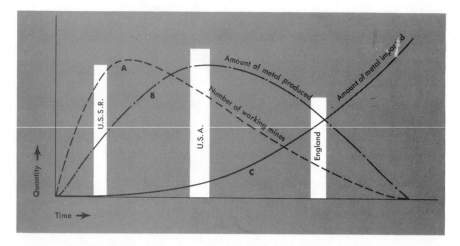

FIG. 6-5 Traditional stages in mine development, metal production, and imports in industrial countries. Curve A, which represents the number of working mines, rises rapidly as a new country is prospected, but it declines when the rate of mine exhaustion exceeds the discovery rate. Curve B, which represents metals produced, also rises and falls as mines are worked and eventually exhausted. Curve C, representing metals imported, rises exponentially and expresses the increasing inability of a country to meet its own needs. The approximate present positions of three industrial countries are indicated. With traditional development, each country moves along the time axis from left to right. For example, England was in about the position of the U.S.A. in the late nineteenth century, at which time the U.S.A. was at about the same stage of development as the U.S.S.R. is today.

ago, the mines that still operate in the portion of Europe formerly embraced by the Roman Empire are all in mineralized areas known and exploited by the Romans. The only exceptions are deposits of metals such as aluminum and chromium, which the Romans did not know how to use. Despite close settlement and keen prospecting by members of a society aware of the importance of metals, no totally new mineral districts were found during a period of almost 2,000 years. History suggests that this pattern is one that will be followed by all countries. Certainly it is apparent in the United States, where new discoveries are now rare in the densely populated, long-settled eastern states, and where the discovery rate in the western states is declining noticeably. The pattern is also apparent from the reliance on imported sources in selected countries (Table 6-2).

As the inadequately prospected areas of the world diminish, we will be forced to develop more sensitive means of searching beneath soil and rock covers and to develop criteria for narrowing the areas of search to those few selected spots on the earth where the probability of finding ores is greatest. How successful this will be is a great unknown. Many ore deposits tend to form at the earth's surface or within a few thousand meters of it. Scientific observation, therefore, leads to the prediction that the number of ore deposits waiting to be found will not increase with depth and will probably decrease.

Table 6-2 Reliance on imports of selected metals for U.S.A. and U.S.S.R. in 1982, Japan and countries of the European Economic Community (E.E.C.) in 1981. 100% means complete reliance on external sources, 0% means all needs are satisfied by internal production. Japan and the E.E.C. rely very heavily on imports, the U.S.A. is intermediate, and the U.S.S.R. is almost self-sufficient.

	U.S.A.	JAPAN	E.E.C.	U.S.S.R.
Niobium	100%	100%	100%	0%
Manganese	99	97	99	0
Bauxite (aluminum)	97	100	86	38
Tantalum	90	100	100	0
Chromium	88	99	97	0
Platinum	85	98	100	0
Nickel	75	100	100	0
Tin	72	96	92	24
Silver	59	58	93	18
Zinc	53	53	81	0
Tungsten	48	68	100	14
Gold	43	96	99	0
Iron ore	36	99	90	0
Vanadium	14	78	100	0
Copper	7	99	99	0
Lead	0	73	74	0

(After U.S. Bureau of Mines).

This is hardly a comforting thought. We need more exact and more certain prospecting methods, particularly where buried ores are concerned. We also need much more work leading to the identification of unconventional potential resources of scarce metals. Success or failure in these areas will directly determine our future use of scarce metals. Interestingly, some promising research that focuses on the problem of exploring the crust in depth has already commenced in several countries. Seismic techniques are being employed to study the overall structure of the crust, and a very deep drill hole has been drilled in the U.S.S.R. Expanded use of both techniques will almost certainly help in the discovery of large, deeply buried ore deposits.

CLASSIFICATION OF DEPOSITS

Mineral deposits form because something serves as a concentrating and transporting medium for the minerals found in the deposits. The five principal concentrating agents, which are just as effective for geochemically abundant elements as they are for the geochemically scarce ones, provide a convenient basis for classifying mineral deposits (Table 6-3). We have already discussed some types of ore deposits in Chapter 5. Examples are magmatic segregation deposits of vanadium-rich magnetite, residual deposits of aluminum, iron and manganese minerals, placer deposits of rutile, and chemical sedimentary deposits of iron and manganese minerals.

Two additional classes of deposit are extremely important for the concentration of many of the geochemically scarce metals. The first involves magma as a concentrating agent. Certain magmas, such as those which form granites, frequently have several percent of water dissolved in them. When a granite magma crystallizes, most of the crystals are anhydrous, so an increasingly water-rich residue remains; valuable metals such as lithium, beryllium, tin, niobium, tantalum, and uranium became concentrated in this residue. If the crystallization process takes place deep in the crust, the water-rich residue may migrate and form small igneous satellite masses. The small satellite bodies are usually very coarse-grained. These *pegmatites* are important sources of certain scarce metals. Because pegmatites commonly form deep in the crust— usually deeper than 10 kilometers—we only observe them at the surface following uplift and very extensive erosion. Pegmatites have been discovered in most countries of the world. Some of the most important are in the northern Appalachians, the southern Sierra Nevada, Canada, Brazil, the countries of west and central Africa, and western Australia.

Table 6-3 Classification of the major classes of mineral deposits on the basis of the concentrating agent.

Concentrating Agent	Class of deposit	Example mineral or metal concentrated
Magma	Pegmatite	Niobium, Beryllium
	Carbonatite	Niobium, Tantalum
	Magmatic segregate	Platinum, Nickel, Chromium
Hot, aqueous, fluid; usually a brine	Hydrothermal	Copper, Lead, Zinc, Silver, Gold, Molybdenum, Tin
Sea or lake water	Marine Evaporite	Sodium Chloride, Potassium Chloride
	Lake Evaporite	Borax, Sodium Carbonate
	Chemical Sediment	Iron, Manganese
Flowing surface waters	Stream Placer	Gold, Diamond
	Marine Placer	Ilmenite, Rutile, Zircon, Diamond
Rainwater	Residual	Nickel, Aluminum

Another important but rare kind of magma consists largely of molten calcite ($CaCO_3$). The origin of carbonate magmas remains in question, but when intruded into the crust, the magmas crystallize to bodies of rock called *carbonatites,* within which important concentrations of the minerals of niobium and tantalum are often found, together with some of the richest deposits of a group of elements known as the *rare earths.* Carbonatites have been discovered on all continents, but the most important bodies discovered so far are in Canada, the United States (especially for the rare earths), South Africa, and Brazil.

The second important class of deposits—indeed the most important of all classes where deposits of scarce metals are concerned—are hydrothermal deposits. These form because heated waters containing some dissolved salts—especially sodium chloride ($NaCl$)—are effective solvents for certain of the sulfide and oxide ore minerals. The water in a hydrothermal solution may be released by a cooling magma through a process similar to that which forms pegmatites, or it may originate on the surface as seawater or rainwater and then trickle down cracks and fractures to great depths in the rocky crust, there to be heated and become a hydrothermal fluid. The chemistry of hydrothermal solutions is controlled by the rocks with which they are in contact. For this reason, the solutions do not always retain the distinctive chemical compositions with which they start. Rather, as the fluids move through the crust they sometimes cool or undergo chemical reactions that cause them to deposit most of their dissolved mineral load, thereby forming a hydrothermal deposit. Tiny samples of hydrothermal solutions are often trapped as inclusions in imperfections in the deposited crystals (Fig. 6-6).

Hydrothermal fluids flow and reach so many different geological settings that geologists tend to classify hydrothermal deposits on the basis of their geological settings. A schematic diagram showing some of the most important settings is shown in Fig. 6-7. In order to appreciate both the importance of the diversity of ways mineral deposits form and the importance of hydrothermal deposits, we turn next to discussions of specific groupings of geochemically scarce elements.

CLASSIFICATION OF SCARCE METALS

When scarce metals form mineral deposits, the minerals in them have distinctive properties and compositions, on the basis of which they can be grouped into three categories. The first, which includes copper, lead, and zinc, commonly form *sulfide minerals.* The second category, which includes gold and platinum, commonly occur as *native metals.* The third, which includes tungsten, tantalum, tin, beryllium, and uranium, commonly form *oxide* and *silicate minerals.* Some overlap occurs—tin, for example, forms both sulfide and oxide minerals—but the groupings are based on the major and most important minerals.

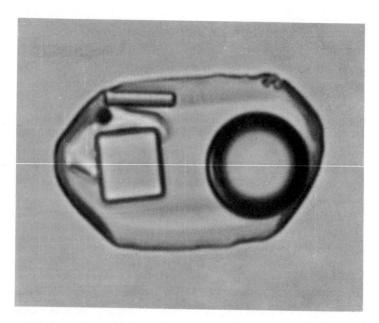

FIG. 6-6 Inclusion of a saline ore fluid trapped in a crystal of quartz as it grew in a hydrothermal vein. The tiny inclusion, only five thousandths of a centimeter long, was filled with a homogeneous liquid at the moment of trapping. Since the liquid was trapped, it has cooled and contracted, forming the round vapor bubble on the right, and salts that were in solution at the higher temperatures have crystallized out. (Courtesy Edwin Roedder.)

FIG. 6-7 Schematic diagram illustrating the most important geological settings for hydrothermal ore deposits. Hydrothermal solutions can arise from water from several different sources.

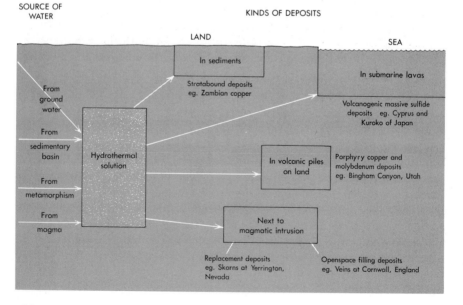

SCARCE METALS FORMING SULFIDE DEPOSITS

The number of scarce metals that are concentrated principally in sulfide deposits is large—copper, lead, zinc, nickel, molybdenum, silver, arsenic, antimony, bismuth, cadmium, cobalt, and mercury, along with numerous rarer ones that occur largely or solely as atomic substitutes for other scarce metals. We can discuss only the most important of the metals.

Copper

Copper, a metal used since antiquity, is now the workhorse of the electrical industry because it is such an excellent conductor. Copper deposits are widespread, but most of them are hydrothermal deposits containing a million metric tons or less of copper. A million tons is small for purposes of modern mining, but such deposits are often extremely rich and may exceed 10 percent copper. Until the turn of the twentieth century, such deposits accounted for most of the copper produced in the world, and because of the high cost of working small deposits by underground mines, the lowest-grade ores that could profitably be mined were about 3 percent. Although copper is still mined on all continents, production from small deposits has continually declined in importance as the discovery and exploitation of large, low-mining-cost deposits, such as the *porphyry copper deposits,* have proceeded.

Prophyry copper ore deposits are large, low-grade hydrothermal deposits; they contain at least 5 million metric tons of ore, and often vastly larger amounts that usually average less than 2 percent copper. The dominant copper minerals are chalcocite (Cu_2S) and/or chalcopyrite ($CuFeS_2$), and they are so evenly distributed that large-volume, and consequently inexpensive, mining practices can be employed. The usual mining system involves the digging of huge open pits (Fig. 6-8); the very large scale upon which mining operations are conducted has allowed the mining of ore to levels as low as about 0.38 percent in some of the newest mines (Fig. 6-9). Porphyry copper deposits are typically associated with igneous rocks that have a distinctive texture called porphyritic—large feldspar or quartz crystals set in a matrix of fine-grained minerals. The deposits are also characteristically contained in large volumes of rock that have been shattered, sheared, faulted, or somehow broken up on a fine scale, and through which mineralizing fluids have found easy passage. The shattering and mineralization may be in the intrusive rock, in the surrounding rocks, or both, and are apparently caused by violent, volcanic forces, because it is now recognized that the place where porphyry deposits form is below sites of volcanism and most commonly below the cones of *stratovolcanoes* (Fig. 6-10). Examples of stratovolcanoes are to be found in the volcanoes of the Aleutians, the Andes, Japan, Mexico, the Cascade Range, and the Philippines. Volcanic structures are readily eroded, and it is likely that many former porphyry copper deposits have been eroded away. The deposits that remain tend to be geologically young—most are less than 200 million

FIG. 6-8 Aerial photograph of the Morenci Open Pit from which the Phelps Dodge Corporation mines the porphyry copper deposit at Morenci, Arizona. The size of the pit can be gauged from buildings visible on the left rim of the pit. (Courtesy of Phelps Dodge Corporation.)

years old and a few are younger than 2 million years. They are also commonly observed to be much more abundant, or even totally confined, within limited geographic regions. Such a deposit-rich region is commonly called a *metallogenic province* (Fig. 6-11). The distinctive metallogenic province within which the porphyry coppers are found in the Americas is nearly parallel to the con-

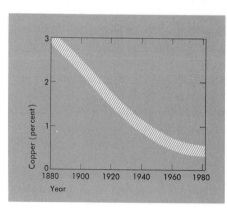

FIG. 6-9 The minimum grade of copper ores that can be profitably worked has decreased steadily with the discovery of large, low-mining-cost deposits and the development of ever larger and more efficient machines. The same trend has not been observed for all metals, possibly because deposits amenable to mass mining methods have not been found. (After U.S. Bureau of Mines.)

FIG. 6-10 Idealized section through a stratovolcano showing convection cells of hydrothermal solution, the limits of hydrothermally altered rocks, and the location of a mineralized zone in which a porphyry copper deposit is forming. (Adapted after Sillitoe, 1973.)

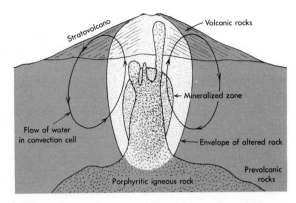

verging margins of the moving crustal plates, because the formation of stratovolcanoes is apparently a result, directly or indirectly, of magma formation in the sinking slab of lithosphere along a subduction zone.

The first porphyry copper to be recognized is still worked at Bingham Canyon, Utah. It is now the largest copper producer in the U.S.A.; D. C. Jackling and R. C. Gemmell were greeted with skepticism when they proposed the idea—revolutionary in 1899—of bulk mining low-grade ores, but their proposal was successful. By 1907 a mill had been built that was capable of han-

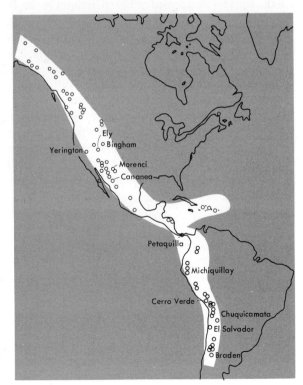

FIG. 6-11 Porphyry copper deposits in the Americas define a remarkable metallogenic province that parallels the western continental boundary. Another belt of porphyry coppers is now being exposed by prospecting in the Pacific Islands.

dling the then huge production of 6,000 metric tons per day. Its daily capacity now exceeds 110,000 metric tons! Several hundred porphyry copper deposits have now been discovered; although principally clustered in the Americas, they have been discovered in the U.S.S.R., in Iran, in Yugoslavia, and most recently in the Philippines, New Guinea, and adjacent Pacific islands. It is very likely that new deposits are forming today beneath some of the world's active stratovolcanoes, and, unlikely as it may seem, there are now plans afoot to drill into some active volcanoes to find out; it seems most unlikely that we will ever mine into the side of an active volcano, however.

A second major type of copper deposit, commonly called *stratiform,* is apparently formed either by the deposition of copper-rich chemical sediment or by chemical replacements in shales soon after they were deposited. Stratiform deposits—so called because they are confined to individual sedimentary horizons and are closely conformable to the sedimentary layering—are known from several geological ages and have a wide geographic distribution. Each stratiform deposit has features somewhat different from others in the class. Copper-rich sediments are not known to be forming today, and the process by which copper minerals are introduced into newly deposited sediments has not been observed. Direct observations cannot, therefore, provide answers to the many puzzles that still surround their origins.

The longest-worked and probably the most famous stratiform deposits in the world were formed in Permian times in the area now occupied by central Europe. The deposits are also among those least altered by metamorphism, so they are also some of the most informative concerning the origin of stratiform deposits. During Permian times, about 250 million years ago, a sedimentary bed of organic-rich muds now containing an unusually high concentration of copper, lead, and zinc sulfides, formed over an area of 50,000 square kilometers in the shallow Zechstein sea (Fig. 6-12). The mud, now consolidated to a shale which is rarely more than 60 centimeters thick and is called the *Kupferschiefer,* has not been uniformly mineralized, for the copper minerals occur with lead and zinc minerals, and the ores are strongly concentrated in small areas in the eastern and central parts of the basin—in East Germany and Poland. It is unclear whether the sulfides precipitated from seawater with

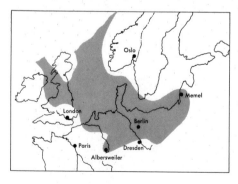

FIG. 6-12 Extent of the shallow Zechstein sea, in which the thin sedimentary bed now known as the Kupferschiefer was laid down during the Permian period. (After R. Brinckmann, 1960.)

the muds, or whether they were introduced during the period immediately following burial, when many chemical and physical changes were taking place in the enclosed organic and mineral matter. There is a good deal of evidence to suggest that the original Kupferschiefer contained only fine-grained iron sulfide grains. Some time after burial a brine carrying small amounts of copper, lead, and zinc chlorides apparently flowed through the very porous, sandy bed that underlies the Kupferschiefer, and in this way came into contact with and replaced the iron sulfides with the minerals we now find, much as an iron nail in a copper chloride solution is slowly transformed to a copper nail.

Since the formation of the ores, the Kupferschiefer has only been slightly changed by low-grade metamorphism. There are a number of similar deposits in Precambrian sediments. Most of these have been more intensively metamorphosed, so that evidence bearing on their origin is even more ambiguous. In the United States the most important deposit of this type is in the White Pine area of Michigan. The deposit has many features in common with the Kupferschiefer, including an extensive, coarse-grained bed beneath the ore horizon. Careful studies of the White Pine deposit have clearly proven that the ore is secondary or postdepositional in origin; the fluids responsible for the replacement probably came from a deep basin filled with basaltic lavas that is now partly under Lake Superior. The deposits of the Dzhezhazgan-Karsakpay area of Kazakhstan are also of considerable importance, but the most remarkable deposits of the type occur in a region of exceedingly rich deposits known as the *Zambian Copper Belt*. These extraordinary deposits occur in sediments that were deposited along ancient shorelines about 700 million years ago. The deposits form an elongate zone (Fig. 6-13) that has two distinct parts, a northern one in Zaire and a southern one in Zambia, which is one of the most richly mineralized regions in the world. Deposits in the Zambian Copper

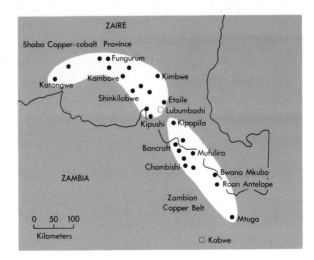

FIG. 6-13 The Zambian Copper belt and adjacent Shaba Copper-Cobalt province in Zaire contain a remarkable series of stratabound copper deposits. Deposits in the Zambian Copper Belt are contained in sediments laid down along an ancient Precambrian shoreline. Those in Zaire are similar in age, but are not shoreline sediments.

Belt are similar to stratiform deposits in other regions in that details of their origins are surrounded by controversy.

More than 50 percent of the world's copper production comes from porphyry deposits, while an estimated 20 percent comes from stratiform deposits, principally those in Zambia. The remainder comes from a great variety of other deposits that are widely distributed and that afford most countries at least a small copper production. The most important class of deposits, in addition to those already referred to, are called *volcanogenic massive sulfide deposits.* The name is descriptive—the deposits are hydrothermal in origin and occur in volcanic rocks that studies have shown are almost entirely of submarine origin. The origin of the deposits appears closely related to the origin of Algoma-type iron deposits (Chap. 5), but in the case of the scarce metals the deposits consist very largely of the sulfide minerals of copper, lead, zinc, and iron (hence the term *massive*). The deposits are often very rich, but unfortunately they tend, on average, to be somewhat smaller than either porphyry or stratiform deposits. Volcanogenic massive sulfide deposits are widely distributed in both time and space, and modern ones have recently been observed forming on the seafloor along the East Pacific Rise. There, at sites of active volcanism, seawater penetrates piles of hot seabed lavas, reacts with the lavas and extracts metals such as iron, copper, and zinc, then rises convectively to the sea as a plume of hot brine. When the hot plume meets cold seawater, the dissolved metals precipitate as sulfides on the seafloor to form a massive sulfide deposit.

In 1982, 56 countries produced copper and sold it on the world market. Because of the overwhelming importance of porphyry deposits and the important role played by stratiform ores, nine countries account for fully 75 percent of the world's production (Table 6-4).

With an annual production close to 8 million tons of copper and with

Table 6-4 Leading copper-producing countries and their reserves, 1982.

Country	Production (metric tons)	Reserves (metric tons)
Chile	1,190,000	97,000,000
U.S.A.	1,100,000	90,000,000
U.S.S.R.	950,000	36,000,000
Canada	640,000	32,000,000
Zambia	540,000	34,000,000
Zaire	480,000	30,000,000
Peru	350,000	32,000,000
Poland	340,000	13,000,000
Australia	250,000	16,000,000
47 other countries	1,940,000	131,000,000
	7,780,000	511,000,000

(After U.S. Bureau of Mines).

rapidly rising consumption curves, we must ask what the future of copper is apt to be. Reserves are large, as shown in Table 6-4, and potential resources must be a good deal larger still, but with a consumption doubling period of about 15 years, the world will need several hundred million metric tons of new copper by the year 2000 alone. What, then, are the potential resources? They are exceedingly difficult to evaluate because we must guess what deposits might be found in the future, and as we have seen, the past record is not encouraging unless new country can be prospected. New deposits will, of course, be found, and some existing ones will prove larger than presently thought. Through such discoveries the known reserves of copper almost doubled between 1972 and 1982. Even so, many specialists have been unwilling to raise their estimates of the amount of copper still to be found in conventional deposits to much more than a billion metric tons. By rough rule of thumb, this is equivalent to finding about as many new deposits as we have already found throughout all of history. Also, the richest deposits left to be discovered might lie in the vast spaces of the U.S.S.R. east of the Urals, in South America, or deeply buried beneath younger rocks in regions such as the southwestern portions of the United States.

Potential resources of copper from unconventional sources are even more difficult to evaluate. The copper content of manganese nodules in the deep oceans is sufficiently high—in places as much as 2 percent—so that the nodules may reach the status of ore within the present decade. Estimates of total recoverable tonnages from nodules are little more than wild guesses, but if 10 percent of the estimated 2×10^{12} metric tons of nodules on the floor of the Pacific yield 0.5 percent copper, the total would be 10^9 metric tons—equal to the sum of all reserves and potential resources. Other potential resources are less obvious. Below a grade of about 0.1 percent, copper tends to be present in rocks by atomic substitution in silicate minerals. Continual lowering of the mining grade, therefore, will bring us to the mineralogical barrier, and surmounting that barrier will require radical new technologies and a great deal of energy. The curve in Fig. 6-9 has a limit, and its indefinite projection is not something on which to place our hopes for the future. The outlook for copper is therefore very good for the next 25 years or so, and possibly even longer through recycling, but is uncertain on a longer scale. Rising prices may make it possible to surmount the technological and energy barriers perceived ahead, but prognostication of uncertainty for copper is not unique. Most scarce metals suffer from the same problem.

Lead and Zinc

Lead and zinc are discussed together because their ore minerals commonly occur together, and for each metal a single mineral species, galena (PbS) and sphalerite (ZnS) respectively, accounts for most of the world's production. Lead is used principally for storage batteries and for lead tetraethyl, an antiknock additive to gasoline, but also finds wide usage in the construction industry, in certain exterior paints, ammunition, and the electrical industry. Zinc, used principally as a component of brass until the nineteenth century, has many uses today, but more than 50 percent of production is consumed in the preparation of alloys for die-cast products and in anticorrosion treatment of iron and steel.

Like deposits of copper ores, those of lead and zinc occur in three very different ways: as hydrothermal deposits of two quite different kinds, and as stratiform deposits. In each case, the ores tend to be rich but confined in size, so that costly underground mining procedures are usually necessary for recovery. Large, low-grade types of deposits analogous to the porphyry coppers have not been discovered.

One important class of hydrothermal deposits, especially for zinc, is volcanogenic massive sulfide deposits. They are very similar to the deposit type described under copper in that they are a product of submarine volcanism; many massive sulfide deposits, such as the famous *kuroko* ores of Japan, are mined for copper, lead, and zinc. One particularly important and unusual variety of hydrothermal deposit, famous for yielding lead and zinc but practically no copper, is known as the *Mississippi Valley type,* after the remarkable metallogenic province stretching from Oklahoma and Missouri to southern Wisconsin and coinciding with much of the drainage basin of the Mississippi River system. Deposits of similar affinity have been identified in several parts of Europe, northern Africa, northern Australia, the U.S.S.R., and, most recently, Canada's Northwest Territory. Indeed, Canada's Pine Point deposit is one of the largest ever discovered, and may belong in the same metallogenic province as the deposits in the United States.

Mississippi Valley deposits occur principally as replacement bodies in limestones of many ages. Solutions carrying the scarce metals apparently dissolved the limestone and slowly deposited the galena and sphalerite that often form large and beautiful crystals (Fig. 6-14). The deposits are usually far from any obvious igneous activity, and a controversy of long standing surrounds the source of solutions. In recent years it has been established, from the analysis of fluids in fluid inclusions, that the solutions were brines with close affinities to those from some oil fields. This information, when combined with the knowledge that Mississippi Valley-type deposits occur around the edges of deep sedimentary basins, is strong evidence that the solutions were somehow driven out of the basins as they were filled with sediments and as these were compacted. It has not been proven that the deposit type is forming today, but it is quite likely that it is, and that oil drillers have already drilled into, but have not recognized, reservoirs of ore fluids.

An increasingly large production of lead and zinc ores has come from stratiform deposits; as with the stratiform copper deposits, the origins of the lead and zinc ores are controversial. The clearest example of a stratiform deposit is again the Kupferschiefer, where the deeper parts of the Zechstein basin apparently favored the accumulation of lead and zinc sulfides rather than of

FIG. 6-14 Large, well-formed crystals of galena (PbS) from the Mississippi Valley type deposits near Picher, Oklahoma suggest that crystal growth was slow and that the frequent shattering characteristically associated with many hydrothermal deposits was absent. The cubes of galena in this photograph are 5 centimeters across.

copper. Although the ores are low in grade, the Kupferschiefer has been worked for both lead and zinc in many places. Like copper deposits, most of the stratiform lead-zinc ores are Precambrian and are now so changed by metamorphism that evidence of their origin has been obliterated. One very large deposit, the Sullivan body, occurs at Kimberly in British Columbia, but the three largest deposits of the class are all in Australia. The first, called the H.Y.C. deposit, is essentially unmetamorphosed and occurs in the far northern part of the country near the McArthur River. The H.Y.C. has many features of a primary sediment, but close examination again shows that the ores could just as well have been formed by reactions between circulating brines and an organic-rich shale rich in iron sulfide. The second deposit is at Broken Hill in the arid western part of New South Wales, and the third is at Mt. Isa, several hundred kilometers to the north in Queensland. Broken Hill and Mt. Isa not only are two of the largest ore deposits known, but also are among the richest. At Broken Hill, ores containing more than 20 percent each of lead and zinc are known.

The world's production of both lead and zinc is dominated by the same five countries (Table 6-5). Reserves reported for both metals are probably not accurate because some countries, such as the U.S.S.R., do not provide the needed information, and in most countries the assessment of ore that will only be mined many years hence is not carried out. Potential resources that are equal in quality and quantity to the reported reserves will almost certainly be developed in the course of normal mining development in many existing deposits as well as in new deposits discovered over the last 10 years. Beyond this

Table 6-5 Leading lead- and zinc-producing countries and their resources, 1981. (The U.S.S.R. does not release figures for production of these metals but almost certainly ranks among the leading producers.)

Country	LEAD Production (metric tons)	LEAD Resources (metric tons)	ZINC Production (metric tons)	ZINC Resources (metric tons)
U.S.A.	510,000	25,000,000	300,000	51,000,000
Australia	450,000	23,000,000	620,000	24,000,000
Canada	335,000	22,000,000	1,165,000	62,000,000
Peru	210,000	4,000,000	535,000	7,000,000
Mexico	155,000	5,000,000	230,000	3,000,000
World Total	3,450,000	146,000,000	6,160,000	243,000,000

(After U.S. Bureau of Mines).

point, however, the situations for both lead and zinc are similar to that for copper—with a marked exception. Potential resources of low-grade and unconventional sources of zinc have been identified in certain rocks associated with salt domes and in some organic-rich shales, but similar resources have not been reported for lead. The short-term future therefore seems secure for lead and zinc, while the long-term picture is hopeful for zinc but very uncertain for lead.

Nickel

Nickel, used almost entirely as an alloying metal in the production of special products such as stainless steel and high-temperature and electrical alloys, is largely a product of late nineteenth- and twentieth-century technology. Smelting and working the metal is so difficult that old German miners, who confused the similar-looking copper and nickel sulfide ores, called it kupfernickel after "Old Nick" who supposedly bewitched the copper (kupfer) ore and thus made it impossible to handle. The frustrations of these miners live on in our use of the word nickel.

There are only two important classes of deposits from which nickel is recovered. The first, accounting for the large Canadian, Russian, and Australian productions (Table 6-6), is from the mineral pentlandite, which commonly occurs in deposits formed by magmatic segregation.

The second class of deposit is found in the residual weathering zones formed over certain igneous rocks in tropical and semitropical regions. We previously used the example of nickel substitution in olivine. Weathering releases the trapped nickel to surface waters, and under some conditions it is reprecipitated as relatively insoluble nickel silicates (Fig. 6-15), such as garnierite ($H_4Ni_3Si_2O_9$), a mineral named for the Frenchman Garnier who first

Table 6-6 Leading nickel-producing countries and their reserves, 1981.

Country	Production (metric tons)	Reserves (metric tons)
Canada	176,600	7,800,000
U.S.S.R.	174,000	7,300,000
New Caledonia	86,000	13,600,000
Australia	82,000	5,100,000
Cuba	42,500	3,100,000
Philippines	33,900	5,200,000
World Total	784,500	56,100,000

(After U.S. Bureau of Mines).

discovered the rich nickel ores of this type in New Caledonia. Beneficiation, which is so costly to man, has thus been effected by nature in a slow, long-continued weathering process.

Although quite pure deposits of garnierite may be formed in this fashion beneath rather lean lateritic cappings, it is more common for tropical weathering to produce an iron-rich laterite in which the concentration of nickel only reaches a level of about 1 percent. Low-grade deposits of this kind are wide-

FIG. 6-15 Chemical weathering of nickeliferous rocks, such as peridotite, released nickel trapped in the olivine; the olivine was then redeposited in the form of minerals such as garnierite. Residual ores of this kind are worked in New Caledonia and Cuba. (After E. de Chétalat, *Bull. Soc. Geol. France,* Sér. 6e, Vol. XVII, 1967, p. 129, Fig. 4.)

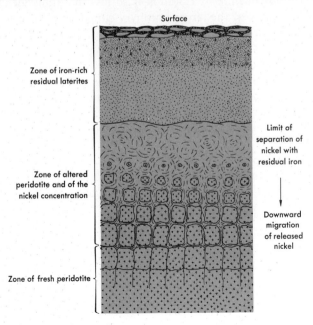

spread in the tropics, and nickeliferous laterites that have potential resources in the hundreds of millions of metric tons have been discovered in Cuba, the Philippines, Greece, Borneo, and other parts of the world. Although this class of deposit is mainly worked in Oregon in the United States, in New Caledonia, and in Cuba at the present time, the laterites constitute our largest known potential resource of nickel, and together with the large segregation deposits they appear to be adequate to meet our demand for nickel far into the future.

Molybdenum

Molybdenum, like nickel, is a metal used mainly as an alloying element in steels, to which it imparts toughness and resilience. Molybdenum first gained widespread importance when it was used in steels for armor plate and armor-piercing shells during World War I. It now has a wide variety of uses, particularly in alloys in which resistance to wear and retention of strength at high temperatures are required.

One mineral, molybdenite (MoS_2), is the source of most of the world's molybdenum, but because molybdenite has a highly erratic distribution, it is difficult to estimate accurately the world's resources of molybdenum. A significant fraction—approximately 25 percent of the world's current molybdenum production—is derived as a by-product of porphyry copper mining. The molybdenum content of porphyry copper ores is low—in the range of 0.01 to 0.04 percent—but such large tonnages of ore are processed and the cost of concentrating molybdenite by flotation is so low that molybdenum recovery is profitable at many of the larger porphyry copper mining operations.

The site of the major production and future resources of molybdenum is a series of deposits that have many geological similarities to porphyry copper deposits and are often called stockwork molybdenum deposits (because the molybdenite is confined to a myriad of tiny fractures that form a stockwork throughout the porphyry). The deposits are found in a metallogenic province stretching from northern Mexico to Alaska, parallel to and probably part of the same metallogenic province in which the porphyry coppers are found (Fig. 6-11).

One of the deposits, at Climax, Colorado, supplied half of the world's production for 50 years; today, together with the nearby Henderson deposit, it supplies about 40 percent of the world's molybdenum. Such heavy dependence on two ore deposits may seem unwise, but the dependence is now being eased by large-scale mining operations at other deposits in Canada and the United States.

The 1982 current world production rate of molybdenum was approximately 90,000 metric tons. With reserves of 6,000,000 metric tons of molybdenum, plus very large potential resources in the U.S.A. alone, we are unlikely to face a resource problem with molybdenum supplies for many years to come.

Silver

The widespread attention paid to silver is derived from its use in currency, jewelry, and monetary speculation. A real shortage is arising from industrial consumption, however, with the photographic and electrical industries consuming an ever larger share of a supply that cannot be easily expanded to satisfy demands.

Shortly after Columbus discovered the Americas, the great silver bonanzas of Central and South America were found. To the present day, deposits in the Cordilleran chain, stretching from Alaska to Tierra del Fuego, have remained a major source of silver. For many decades, and still today, 55 percent or more of the silver produced annually comes from countries in the Americas, with most of the remainder coming from Australia and the Soviet Union, and only marginal production from Asia and Africa.

Silver minerals commonly occur in hydrothermal vein deposits. Either they are associated with lead, zinc, and copper minerals, or else the silver itself is carried in the lead and copper minerals by atomic substitution. Only a minor percentage of silver-producing deposits are rich enough to be worked for silver alone, and therein lies the silver problem. Most silver is produced as a by-product of copper, lead, and zinc mining, and its production rate is strictly controlled by the production rates of the associated metals. Although a few new silver deposits have been found in recent years, such a high proportion of newly mined silver is produced as a by-product that silver production has not been able to expand to meet growing needs. With the 1965 decision by the United States Government to withdraw silver from currency, the price of silver rose rapidly, and it will remain high unless large new supplies are found. Such discoveries do not seem likely. Though old mines may be reactivated and formerly uneconomic ores become profitable in the face of rising silver prices, there seems little hope that silver production will grow to meet all demands; rather, it is likely that future uses will have to be curtailed because the limited supply means prices will remain so high that substitute materials will be employed wherever possible.

Other Sulfide-Forming Scarce Metals

The remaining scarce metals that occur principally as sulfides do not warrant separate discussion. Almost without exception, small deposits are widespread and resources seem adequate for foreseeable future needs. The apparent exception is mercury.

Most of the world's mercury production comes from one mineral, the vermillion-colored cinnabar (HgS), which is found erratically distributed in narrow hydrothermal veins in a number of volcanic areas. The known deposits are all shallow, and most are so small that they were exhausted soon after discovery. The world's current production comes largely from Spain, where the Almaden mine has been producing for more than 2,000 years, from Idria in Yugoslavia, from Algeria, from the United States, and from the U.S.S.R. The once-great deposits of California and Nevada are apparently almost exhausted. Known reserves of mercury are small, and its by-production from other mining activities is limited. Many experts now suspect that it may be the first scarce metal for which available supplies are exhausted; the moment of exhaustion may even be reached in the twentieth century.

SCARCE METALS OCCURRING IN THE NATIVE STATE

Platinoid Metals

The scarce metals occurring in the native state are a less diverse group than those that form sulfide minerals. Platinum, palladium, rhodium, iridium, ruthenium, and osmium, collectively called the *platinoid* elements, always occur together and are concentrated in igneous rocks derived from mantle magmas. The abundance levels of the platinoids are all low—platinum and palladium, the most abundant of the group, are only present in the crust to an extent of 0.0000005 percent; the others are even less abundant. However, the platinoid abundance in mantle rocks is noticeably higher though not sufficiently so for the rocks to be considered potential resources of platinoids. The most important way that platinoid metals are concentrated into ore deposits is through magmatic segregation of nickel, copper, and iron sulfides. As the sulfide compounds form and sink to the floor of the magma chamber, they act as atomic collectors and sweep the platinoids out of magmatic solution. In mining magmatic segregation deposits for copper and nickel, therefore, platinoids are recovered as valuable by-products. Within South Africa's Bushveld Igneous Complex there is a segregation layer called the Merensky Reef, which, although only a few tens of centimeters thick, is so rich that it can be mined for its platinoid content rather than for the nickel and copper it contains.

There is one other important occurrence of platinoids. The metals are essentially unaffected by chemical weathering and are malleable. Thus, grains of these metals do not disintegrate as they are transported and deposited in sediments; being very dense, they concentrate in placers (Fig. 6-16). Where the sediment source area contains suitable igneous rocks, as in the Ural Mountains in the U.S.S.R., important placer concentrations of platinoids can develop.

Reserves of platinoid elements are quite large compared to the small production (Table 6-7), but they are very unevenly distributed; most are in the Bushveld Complex and in the U.S.S.R. Potential resources are uncertain, but they are probably large. Many layered intrusives, such as the Stillwater Complex in Montana and the Duluth Gabbro in Minnesota, contain large, low-grade potential resources. The main trouble with platinoids is that production

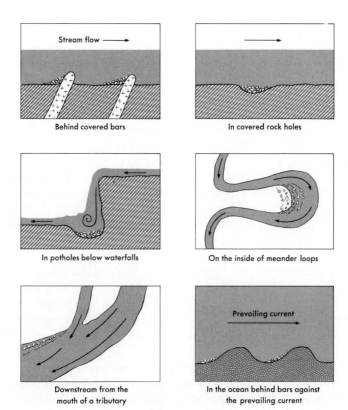

FIG. 6-16 Typical sites of placer accumulations where obstructing or deflecting barriers allow faster-moving waters to carry away the suspended load of light and fine-grained material while trapping denser and coarser particles that are moving along the bottom by rolling or partial suspension. Placers can form wherever there is moving water, although they are most commonly associated with streams.

Table 6-7 Leading Platinoid- and Gold-producing countries, 1982.

| Country | PLATINOIDS* | | GOLD | |
	Production (metric tons)	Reserves (metric tons)	Production (metric tons)	Reserves (metric tons)
U.S.S.R.	108.8	6,220	327	8,400
Rep. of South Africa	80.9	30,200	659	21,800
Canada	5.9	280	56	1,240
U.S.A.	0.2	498	44	3,110
World Total	199.0	37,300	1,275	41,400

*The platinoid elements are grouped because of similar occurrences and uses. Within the group, platinum and palladium each account for about 40 percent of the production and reserves, rhodium 9 percent, iridium 6 percent, ruthenium 4 percent, and osmium 1 percent.

(After U.S. Bureau of Mines).

of low-grade resources may have to be linked to production of other metals such as copper or nickel. Thus, in the future the platinoid situation may become analogous to the present silver situation.

Gold

Gold, unlike the platinoids, is not commonly associated with mantle rocks, but is characteristically associated with igneous rocks formed within the crust. Like sulfide minerals, gold is transported by hydrothermal solutions. Native gold is one of the least soluble substances known, but it can be transported in solution by formation of chloride and sulfide compounds. Gold is commonly found in hydrothermal vein deposits, either associated with sulfide minerals or alone. Very rarely does an ore contain much gold; a rich ore, for example, contains only 0.007 percent gold and yields about 60 grams of gold for every metric ton of rock mined. Much leaner ores than this can be profitably worked, however.

Gold is so resistant to corrosion that it is almost indestructible. Most of the gold ever mined is still available, having been used and reused many times in its passage through history. Some of the gold from Cleopatra's bracelets, for example, may reside in your tooth fillings or wedding band. Gold is also an unusual element in that it forms a separate mineral even at very low concentration levels and is not concealed by atomic substitution to the same extent that many other, even more abundant, elements are. Because gold is widespread in tiny amounts and is indestructible and very dense, it is ideally suited for concentration in placer deposits, from which has come much of the world's production.

Among the most remarkable of all the mineral deposits in the world are the gold deposits of the Witwatersrand district of South Africa. Formed in Precambrian times, about 2.5 billion years ago, the ores are contained in a series of conglomerates—sedimentary rocks consisting of rounded pebbles cemented by a finer-grained matrix. This is exactly the rock type that commonly carries placer concentrations in most parts of the world and in all geologic ages; there the story would end but for the astonishing extent of the Rand ores. Most placer deposits are small, perhaps a few hundred or thousands of meters in extent, and are clearly confined to present or former stream channels. The Rand ores too are apparently localized by what were old channels, but the deposits have been mined along an outcrop length of conglomerates in excess of 400 kilometers, and they have been followed to the limits of practical mining—more than 3.5 kilometers deep. Those who have studied these ores do not propose alternatives to placer deposition, but no one has successfully solved the problem of their great size. They seem to have formed in the marginal parts of either an inland sea or a shallow marine embayment, because the ores are actually in what were formerly shallow water deltas. Closely associated with the gold are grains of uraninite, and as a result the Witwatersrand district is not only the world's largest producer of gold but also one of the largest producers of uranium. Perhaps there are other Rand-type ores; similar gold deposits, though smaller, have been discovered in Brazil, and in Canada similar uranium deposits have been discovered in the Blind River district of Ontario.

First discovered in 1885, the Rand district soon became, and has remained, the world's leading gold producer. In 1982 it accounted for 52 percent of the world's gold production. Although gold production is widespread around the world—71 countries reported some production in 1982—large deposits are rare, and only 4 countries account for 85 percent of production. One of the largest gold mines in the United States is the Homestake Mine in South Dakota. The deposit is Precambrian in age, has been metamorphosed, and is of uncertain origin. Scientists who have examined the deposit suggest that submarine hot springs deposited gold and associated scarce metals into the sedimentary host rocks as they were being deposited, and that the metal was further concentrated into veins and pods during metamorphism. Three gold deposits of an unusual type are mined in Nevada: the Carlin, Cortez, and Getchell mines. Recent discoveries of similar deposits in Nevada and California give hope that more deposits of the same type remain to be found. The deposits are hydrothermal; the gold is so fine-grained that it can rarely be seen even under a microscope. Finding new deposits, therefore, calls for very skilled prospecting.

In addition to its widespread monetary use, gold has other uses that continually drive the consumption rate upward. The largest use is in jewelry, but the need for electronic components in computers is rising rapidly, and dental needs present a steady demand. For many years the price of gold was controlled by governmental edicts, but with the establishment of a free world market in 1968, and restoration of rights of private ownership within the United States, the price of gold moved rapidly above $5 a gram. The question of reserves and potential resources must be viewed in light of a rising price. In 1968 the U.S. Bureau of Mines estimated that world reserves of gold ore that could be profitably worked at a price of $4.66 a gram ($145 an ounce) contained approximately 37,000 metric tons of gold. The price of gold soon rose above $4.66 a gram, but world reserves did not increase. The price at the end of 1982 was close to $15 a gram, but world reserves still had not increased significantly. Despite many prospecting successes such as the previously mentioned new deposits in Nevada and California, large increases in reserves of gold ores have not occurred because large, low-grade potential resources of gold have not been identified. Thus, gold may present something of an economic anomaly: The price may rise, but the amount produced may not increase at the same rate.

Scarce Metals Forming Oxide Deposits

With the exception of tin, the scarce metals with affinities for oxygen are all newcomers, and the diverse uses to which they are put reflect the amazingly complex technology we now support. Chromium, tungsten, tantalum, vanadium, and niobium (formerly known as columbium) are principally used as alloying agents in special steels, but they also have other highly specialized uses. For example, a large percentage of the tungsten produced is now used in the manufacture of tungsten carbide (WC), an extremely hard substance used for cutting edges in metal work, in rock drills, and in armor-piercing shells; tantalum has been proven to have the special electronic properties needed for low-power valves, and it offers interesting possibilities for the computers of the future. Uranium, of course, has special properties of its own because energy can be released from the atomic nucleus by controlled fission. Because uses of uranium are those of a fuel rather than of a metal, uranium was separately discussed in Chapter 4.

Chromium

Chromium, the oxide-forming scarce metal with the largest annual production, is an essential alloying metal for steel, and one for which satisfactory substitutes have not been found. Important amounts are also consumed in the chemical industry and in the use of chromite, $(Mg,Fe)Cr_2O_4$, for refractory bricks.

Until the end of the last century, chromium was used only in the chemical industry, principally in the manufacture of pigments. After 1900, however, it gained importance as an alloying element; high-speed tool steels and stainless steels with a chromium base find ever wider application. Chromium is now an essential metal of modern technology.

Chromium is only known to form a single ore mineral, chromite. Supplies of chromite are limited both in abundance and in geographic diversity. Alternative sources of chromium have not been identified.

Chromite deposits form only by magmatic segregation; chromite lends itself to concentration in this manner because it is very dense and crystallizes early in the magmatic cooling cycle (Fig. 6-17). Unfortunately, the kinds of magmas in which chromite forms are characteristic of the mantle and are rare in the crust. Deposits are found, therefore, where fragments of the mantle have reached the surface, or where mantle-generated magmas invade the crust. This happens in two ways. First, fragments from the upper mantle are sometimes torn off and thrust upward along sutures where crustal plates have collided. These mantle fragments commonly contain a type of igneous rock called *peridotites,* and these in turn sometimes contain layers and pods of chromite formed by magmatic segregation. Because peridotite masses are found in the mountain belts formed by collision, they are called *alpine peridotites.* The second way chromite reaches the crust is as a constituent of magmas. We now find the magmas cooled into layered intrusions; chromite may be present in these in rich magmatic cumulates.

Much of the world's past production of chromite has come from alpine peridotites in the Ural Mountains of the U.S.S.R., the mountains of Turkey, the Philippines, Greece, Iran, Yugoslavia, India, and the United States. Unfortunately, the deposits are all small, difficult to locate, and, in many cases,

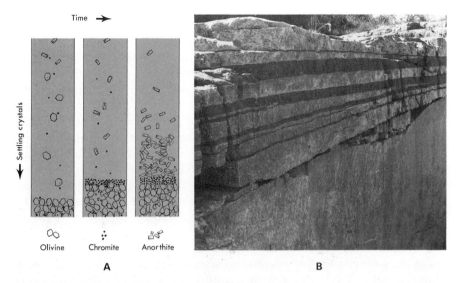

FIG. 6-17 (A) Large, heavy materials settle faster than small, light ones during magmatic segregations, giving rise to marked compositional layering in certain igneous rocks. Chromite, ilmenite, and magnetite are all concentrated in this fashion. (B) Example of layering developed between chromite and anorthosite (white) in the Bushveld Complex, a layered intrusion in South Africa. (B. J. Skinner.)

difficult to mine. Increasingly, therefore, attention has been paid to layered intrusions, and here the reserves are much larger. Most of these are located in Africa. One of the most unusual masses of igneous rocks in the world occurs in South Africa. Known as the Bushveld Complex, and comprised of many different layers of igneous rock, several of which contain chromite, it covers about 60,000 square kilometers and contains high-grade reserves reported in 1982 to be 2.5 billion metric tons of chromite, plus potential resources that may be as large as 10 billion metric tons.

Another large layered intrusion, called the Great Dike, occurs in Zimbabwe; here too, vast rich reserves of chromite are known. It is clear that southern Africa will become even more important in the production of chromite than it is now. This part of the world is now dominating the trade of chromite by supplanting the traditional leader, the U.S.S.R.

Fortunately, layered intrusions have been found on all continents, and most of these contain low-grade potential resources of chromite. An example of such a large, lower-grade resource is the Stillwater Complex, a layered intrusion in Montana which contains most of the potential resources of chromite in the United States. Even though the low-grade potential resources are presently undesirable sources of chromite, many countries could, if they wished, be self-sufficient in this metal. There does not seem to be a danger of chromium shortage in the future. If African supplies are disrupted or cut off for some reason, however, the cost of chromium could rise steeply as lower-grade resources are developed.

Tin and Tungsten

Tin is the only scarce metal of the group, besides chromium, with a large production; it has been used as an alloying agent in bronze for thousands of years. The largest uses today are in the tinplate industry, where tin serves as an anticorrosion coating on iron and steel, and in the production of soft solders.

Tin and tungsten minerals often occur together. Deposits of the metals are often found adjacent to certain igneous rock in the continental crust in so-called *skarn* deposits. These form when granitic rocks come into contact with limestone. The most common ore minerals in the deposits—cassiterite (SnO_2), wolframite ($[Fe,Mn] WO_4$), and scheelite ($CaWO_4$)—are dense and resistant to weathering, so they are readily concentrated in placer deposits. Much of the world's supply, particularly of tin, has come from such secondary concentrations.

Tin and tungsten are both elements for which the availability of future resources is uncertain; their abundances are low and their deposits few. North America, for example, has few tin deposits, but it is more fortunate in its tungsten resources. Most of the world's tin production and the known reserves and potential resources are concentrated in two narrow metallogenic provinces, one that runs from Java, then along the Malayan Peninsula, eastern China, Korea, and into eastern Siberia, and another that runs along the eastern side of the high Andes, in Bolivia and Peru. The major tungsten production and reserves are also restricted geographically; approximately half of the world's production comes from the same east-Asian metallogenic belt that produces much of the world's tin.

Other Oxide-Formers

There are a number of other oxide-forming scarce metals, but the most important are niobium, tantalum, and beryllium, all of which are found concentrated in *pegmatites.* For many years pegmatites served as the only source for niobium, tantalum, and beryllium. In recent years, however, new and unexpected sources have been found for each metal. Niobium and tantalum minerals have been found in many carbonatites, and beryllium silicate has been found as an exceedingly fine-grained and previously overlooked mineral in certain hydrothermally altered lavas in Utah, Nevada, and New Mexico. Although the beryllium mineral is too fine to allow beneficiation, it can be leached by acid solutions and recovered. The Spor Mountains beryllium deposit in Utah has become the largest potential resource of beryllium for the future.

SCARCE METALS IN THE FUTURE

Two points about the scarce metals raise uncertainty for the future. The first concerns the occurrence and distribution of ore deposits—they are limited in size, geographically restricted, and difficult to find. Evaluating potential resources, we find that large, low-grade, unconventional deposits have not been identified for most metals. We cannot even be sure whether or not deposits of any kind are likely to occur in the composition gap between presently minable ores and average crustal rocks. In the case of copper, unconventional resources will be available when the presently exploited deposits are used up. But for metals such as silver, tungsten, and mercury, no alternatives are yet in sight.

The second point concerns use patterns. We use scarce metals at a much faster rate than is prudent, considering their scarcity. If we were to use metals in proportion to their abundances, we would use greatly increased amounts of iron, aluminum, and other geochemically abundant metals, and decreased amounts of geochemically scarce metals. For example, if we were to take the 1981 annual world production of pig iron, about 550 million metric tons, as a base, and if we used other metals in proportion to their geochemical abundances, the consumption rate of copper would have been about 550,000 metric tons; of lead, 95,000 metric tons; and of tin, 14,300 metric tons. In fact, the consumption rates were respectively 15, 35, and 18 times greater. This suggests that rich deposits of most scarce metals will be consumed long before similar deposits of abundant metals. Prices of geochemically scarce metals are likely to rise more rapidly than prices of abundant metals, therefore, and this will probably bring proportional use rates of metals more nearly into line with their proportional abundances.

fertilizer and chemical minerals

. . . the use of chemical fertilizer in 1960 was about six times the level of the 1930's. The additional production flowing from the recent rate of consumption of some 6 to 7 millions tons of plant nutrients per year . . . is roughly equivalent to the yield from some 75 million acres of unfertilized farmland. (H. H. Landsberg, Natural Resources for U.S. Growth, 1964.)

World production (of phosphate rock) has steadily increased, rising to 108, 119, 129, 133 and 138 million metric tons in 1976, 1977, 1978, 1979, and 1980 respectively. With expansion plans expected to be implemented during the 1980's adequate supplies of phosphate rock appear assured for this period. (Minerals Yearbook, Vol I, 1980.)

The term *nonmetallic minerals* is somewhat ambiguous; it is neither a strictly scientific nor an exact economic term. It is widely used, however, and embraces a group of minerals used for purposes other than the metals they contain. The nonmetallic minerals are not readily classified in terms of the crustal abundance of a chemical element; they can, however, be simply classified on the basis of use. First, there are the minerals of primary use for fertilizers and for raw chemicals, accounting for 33 percent of the value of the nonmetallic production. Second, there are the materials for the building and construction industries discussed in Chapter 8.

MINERALS FOR FERTILIZERS

The fertilizer minerals are, without doubt, one of our most vital resources, because they are essential for increasing food production to meet the demands of an expanding population that seeks an ever better standard of living. Plant growth requires many chemical elements. Oxygen and hydrogen (both derived from water) together with carbon (derived from atmospheric carbon dioxide) make up 98 percent of the bulk of living plants. But nitrogen, phosphorus, potassium, calcium, and sulfur are also essential, and for land plants—the source of our food supplies—they are provided largely by the soil. The rate of supply in part determines the rate of plant growth. If they are to have any effect at all, the elements must be supplied in a form that the plant can assimilate. For example, most soils contain 1 percent or more of potassium, but much of this potassium is unavailable to plants because it is locked into insoluble silicate minerals such as feldspars. To enhance growth rates by addition of a potassium fertilizer, we usually add potassium as the sulfate (K_2SO_4) or chloride (KCl), because both compounds are readily soluble. The efficacy of the nitrogenous, phosphatic, and other fertilizers also depends on their solubility, and it is in the form of soluble compounds, or minerals that can readily be rendered soluble, that fertilizer resources are sought.

The most essential fertilizers—the "big three"—are phosphorus, potassium, and nitrogen. These are applied to soils in the approximate weight ratio of 1 to 1.5 to 3, but we must remember that they are not applied as chemical elements but rather as chemical compounds of various kinds. Demand for fertilizers has been climbing very rapidly (Fig. 7-1), and the total world fertilizer consumption is doubling every 10 years. There seems little chance that the demand for fertilizer will decline while the population continues to rise. The most rapid growth in fertilizer use is in countries such as Brazil where large areas of poor soil are being developed for agriculture. Fertilizer reserves

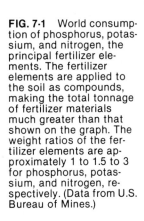

FIG. 7-1 World consumption of phosphorus, potassium, and nitrogen, the principal fertilizer elements. The fertilizer elements are applied to the soil as compounds, making the total tonnage of fertilizer materials much greater than that shown on the graph. The weight ratios of the fertilizer elements are approximately 1 to 1.5 to 3 for phosphorus, potassium, and nitrogen, respectively. (Data from U.S. Bureau of Mines.)

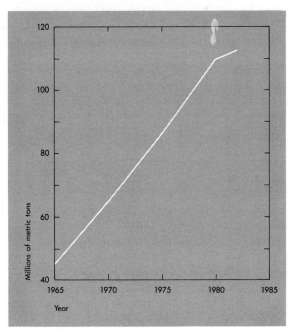

are, fortunately, very large, but with the exception of nitrogen, reserves of materials used at present suffer from the same problems that beset many of the scarce metals—they are geographically restricted (Table 7-1).

Nitrogen

As mentioned in Chapter 2, nitrogen is the principal resource won from the atmosphere. The form in which it is added to the soil is either as a soluble nitrate, such as $NaNO_3$, or, more commonly, as an ammonia compound, such as $(NH_4)_2SO_4$ or NH_4NO_3.

Most synthetic nitrogen compounds are produced either by one of the variants of the Haber-Bosch process—in which nitrogen from the atmosphere and hydrogen (usually from methane, CH_4, in natural gas) are combined under high temperatures and pressures to form ammonia—or as by-products from coke ovens. The process uses a great deal of energy; nitrogen fertilizer plants are one of the most energy- and capital-intensive segments of industry. Nevertheless, nitrogen is the largest contributor to the fertilizer curve in Fig. 7-1. The cost of fertilizers is strongly influenced by the cost of energy. Atmospheric nitrogen is the dominant source of nitrogen for nitrogenous compounds, but a tiny production of natural nitrates from Chilean deposits continues. Although nitrate salts are very soluble, they can accumulate in the soils of Chile's Atacama Desert because there is virtually no rainfall. It is an interesting historical footnote that Chile fought a war against Bolivia and Peru (the so-called

Table 7-1 Production of nitrogen, phosphorus, and potassium compounds, used principally as agricultural fertilizers, 1981. Nitrogen is won from the atmosphere; phosphorus and potassium are mined.

Country	Nitrogen*	Phosphate Rock[†]	Potash[‡]
		(millions of metric tons)	
U.S.A.	14.2	53.6	2.2
U.S.S.R.	12.6	30.9	8.4
China	7.4	5.5	—
India	2.9	0.6	—
Canada	2.2	—	6.8
West Germany	2.0	—	2.6
East Germany	1.2	—	3.5
Morocco	—	19.7	—
Tunisia	—	4.6	—
World Total	71.5	138.6	27.4

*Reported as the amount of contained nitrogen.
[†]The phosphorus content is variable, but averages about 13% by weight.
[‡]Reported as potash, K_2O. The potassium content is 83% by weight.
(After U.S. Bureau of Mines).

War of the Pacific, 1879–1883) in order to control the Atacama nitrate deposits. The deposits ceased to be important when the Haber-Bosch process was invented.

Almost 20 percent of the nitrogen consumed annually is produced in the United States, and half of the total world production is synthesized in just four countries (Table 7-1).

Potassium

Potassium is an abundant element that is widely distributed in virtually insoluble silicate minerals. The soluble potassium minerals are sought for use as fertilizers, and these are almost entirely confined to a class of mineral deposits known as *marine evaporites* that result from the accumulation of salts by evaporation of seawater. Marine evaporites are also of vital importance in the production of other minerals, so we will discuss their origin briefly.

The major elements dissolved in seawater were displayed in Fig. 2-5. They can be recast into the constituents that actually precipitate from seawater by balancing the positively charged cations, such as sodium (Na^{+1}), against the negatively charged anions, such as chlorine (Cl^{-1}), to preserve electrical neutrality (Table 7-2). Sodium chloride is the most abundant constituent; next follow the magnesium salts, then calcium sulfate, and potassium chloride. When water is removed by evaporation, brine becomes increasingly concentrated and finally reaches saturation, first in one salt, then in the others. It is not necessarily the most abundant compound that precipitates first; saturation of the relatively insoluble—and therefore sparse—compounds is usually reached long before saturation of those that are highly soluble.

The first compound to precipitate from evaporating seawater is $CaCO_3$, for which the solubility is extremely low and the amount in solution small

Table 7-2 Major constituents of seawater*

Constituent	Percentage of Total Dissolved Solids
NaCl	78.04
$MgCl_2$	9.21
$MgSO_4$	6.53
$CaSO_4$	3.48
KCl	2.11
$CaCO_3$	0.33
$MgBr_2$	0.25
$SrSO_4$	0.05

*Obtained by recasting the data in Fig. 2–5 into molecular compositions.

relative to NaCl. The next compound, $CaSO_4$*, does not begin to precipitate until the solution has been reduced to 19 percent of the original volume; NaCl, the third compound to precipitate, does so when the residual solution reaches 9.5 percent of the original volume. Precipitation of NaCl, plus a small amount of $CaSO_4$, continues until the brine is reduced to about 4 percent of its original volume; then the first compound to contain magnesium and potassium, a complex salt called polyhalite ($K_2SO_4 \cdot MgSO_4 \cdot 2CaSO_4 \cdot 2H_2O$), begins to precipitate. The amount of NaCl in solution is large to begin with, and considerably more than half of it is precipitated during the reduction in the volume of the solution from 9.5 percent to 4 percent; the thickest layer formed during a single evaporation cycle will therefore be the NaCl layer. The sequence of minerals separating from the final 4 percent of the brine (called the bitterns) is complex and variable, and depends on such factors as the temperature and whether or not the final liquid remains in contact, and hence can react with the earlier-formed crystals. Two of the precipitates found in most sequences are sylvite (KCl) and carnallite ($KCl \cdot MgCl_2 \cdot 6H_2O$), and it is in these late-stage evaporite minerals that most of the world's useful resources of potassium minerals are to be found.

The evaporation of a completely isolated body of seawater would produce the sequence and volume of salts shown in Fig. 7-2. When we examine actual evaporite deposits, these volume relationships are rarely found—the early-formed precipitates, $CaCO_3$ and $CaSO_4$, are relatively much more abundant, and the late-formed precipitates, the K and Mg salts, are rare. The complete evaporation of a body of seawater as deep as the Mediterranean, which has an average depth of about 1,370 meters, would produce only 24 meters of NaCl and a layer of $CaSO_4$ only 1.4 meters thick. However, beds of $CaSO_4$ and NaCl several hundreds of meters thick are known. Evidence from fossils in associated rocks indicates that evaporation occurred in shallow bodies of water. Clearly, there must be some mechanism other than the drying up of an isolated, shallow basin by which such deposits are formed. The common circumstance is to find precipitation in a partially isolated basin from which water is removed by evaporation but into which fresh seawater is continually flowing. There are several geologic circumstances by which this can happen, and they are collectively called *barred basins*. Water flows into the basin over a submerged bar; evaporation of the surface waters continually enriches the basin in dissolved salts because the partially enriched but heavier brine sinks to the bottom and is prevented from recirculating by the restricting bar (Fig. 7-3). The salinity of the basin increases more slowly than it would by direct evaporation of an isolated body, and the brine remains for a long time in the salinity range in which $CaCO_3$ precipitates. It is even possible for the precipitated

---

*Either $CaSO_4$ or $CaSO_4 \cdot 2H_2O$ may precipitate depending on the temperature. Discussion of these two compounds can be found in the section on plaster in Chapter 8.

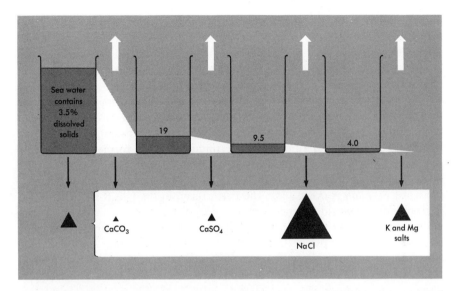

FIG. 7-2 Succession of compounds precipitating from seawater. When evaporation reduces the starting volume to 19 percent, $CaSO_4$ begins to precipitate; at 9.5 percent, NaCl; and so on.

$CaCO_3$ to fill the basin completely to the level of the bar before a salinity is reached that is sufficiently high to cause the precipitation of $CaSO_4$. Similarly, thick beds of $CaSO_4$ may form and the brines may never reach the NaCl stage. The frequency of occurrence and the total thickness of evaporite salts in sedimentary basins around the world decrease in the order $CaCO_3 > CaSO_4 >$ NaCl > K and Mg salts.

At the present time, evaporite deposits are accumulating on every continent. Although high temperatures are not essential for concentration—drying winds can accomplish the same thing in cold climates—most evaporites are formed in a belt between 35 degrees north latitude and 35 degrees south lat-

FIG. 7-3 Diagrammatic cross section of a barred basin. Fresh seawater flows over the bar and is concentrated by evaporation. The dense brine sinks and is prevented from returning to the open sea by the bar. When the brine reaches a sufficiently high salinity, salts precipitate and may eventually fill the basin.

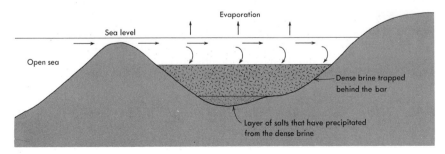

itude. The modern deposits are all small, and there is not at present any large marginal sea with a restricting flow—such as the Baltic, the Mediterranean, or the Black Sea—that fulfills both the morphological and the climatic conditions that are necessary for the formation of a large evaporite deposit. The largest today is probably the Gulf of Kara Bogaz in the U.S.S.R. on the eastern side of the Caspian Sea. As we look at the geological record, however, we find that this is a temporary situation, for marine evaporites are widely spread both in time and in space, and there have been several times in the past when worldwide conditions were much more conducive to the formation of marine evaporites than they are at present. During the Permian period exceptionally thick evaporite sequences were formed in North America and Europe. Indeed, the word *Permian* is taken from the Perm Basin in the U.S.S.R., which contains one of the world's largest evaporite deposits.

Evaporites are our principal source of halite (NaCl, familiar to us as common salt), of gypsum ($CaSO_4 \cdot 2H_2O$), and of potassium salts. In some cases magnesium and less abundant elements are produced as by-products. Halite and gypsum will be discussed later. For the present we will concentrate on potassium compounds.

For many years most of the world relied on the vast Permian evaporite deposits in Germany. It is somewhat ironic that the circumstances of World War I, which closed the German deposits to the United States, should have been responsible for providing the impetus that led to the discovery of even richer deposits of the same type and age in New Mexico. A large, shallow Permian sea deposited a thick section of evaporite salts over an area of at least 160,000 square kilometers that is now New Mexico, Texas, Oklahoma, and Kansas. In a portion of the basin, near Carlsbad, New Mexico, an estimated 4,800 square kilometers of the sequence contain potassium salts in beds that reach 4 meters in thickness. These deposits are among the richest in the world, although they are small by comparison with several others; their reserves and low-grade potential resources of potassium are about 100 million metric tons.

North America has additional large reserves of potassium (Fig. 7-4). A basin of Pennsylvanian age in southeastern Utah and southwestern Colorado, called the Paradox Basin, contains an estimated 12,600 square kilometers of potassium-rich salines. Though much of the deposit is too deep to warrant recovery at present, some is being produced through drill holes by dissolving salts underground, pumping the solution, and recovering the potassium salts through surface evaporation.

In Saskatchewan, Canada, and in nearby North Dakota and Montana in the U.S.A., a huge and as yet incompletely explored resource of potassium salts has been found in the Elk Point and Williston Basins (Devonian period). Published estimates list as much as 37,500 million metric tons of potassium salts as accessible by today's mining methods. These are the largest known resources in the world, but exceedingly large resources are available in the U.S.S.R. too, and in recent years major deposits have been discovered in such

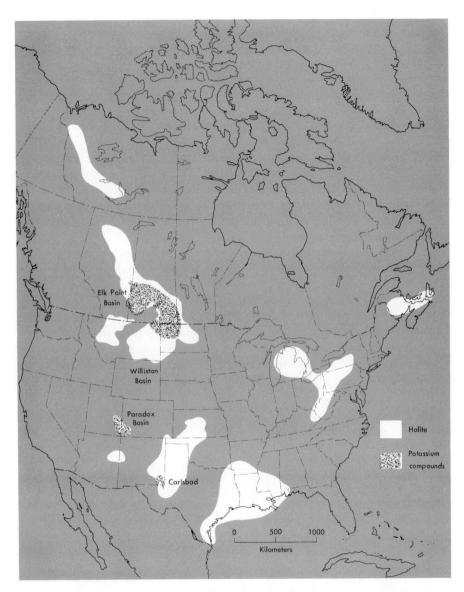

FIG. 7-4 Areas of the United States and Canada underlain by major marine evaporite deposits of halite and potassium salts. (After *U.S. Geol. Surv. Bull.* 1019-J; A. D. Huffman, 1968; P. B. King, 1942; R. J. Hite, 1961; and S. R. L. Handing and H. A. Gorrell, 1967.)

widely scattered places as South America and Southeast Asia. Australia and Antarctica are the only continents where potash evaporites have not yet been discovered. The salts dissolved in the sea are also a nearly inexhaustible potential resource, so even great expansions beyond today's production rates would not seriously threaten supplies of potassium salts.

Phosphorus

The phosphorus cycle appears to be the one most disrupted by intensive land cultivation. Phosphorus is a vital element for many cellular processes in the body. The major store of it is in our skeletons, composed of the mineral *apatite* [$Ca_5(PO_4)_3(OH)$], and this store of phosphorus is not returned to the soils of our crop lands after death; it is therefore necessary to supply it as a fertilizer. The only important source of phosphorus, and the only common phosphate mineral, is apatite; however, apatite is relatively insoluble. It is common practice, therefore, to treat apatite (or *phosphate rock,* as most of the apatite-rich raw materials are called) with dilute acids, usually sulfuric acid (H_2SO_4), to convert apatite into a more soluble material. The chemical reactions that occur when sulfuric acid reacts with apatite are complex; the resulting *superphosphate* contains a high percentage of water-soluble compounds such as $Ca(H_2PO_4)_2$.

Apatite is widespread in trace amounts in most rocks, regardless of whether they are igneous, metamorphic, or sedimentary. Major concentrations of apatite in igneous rocks are known, but they are comparatively rare. One such concentration, on the Kola Peninsula (Fig. 7-5) in the northern Soviet Union, in a rock called syenite, is mined for its apatite content and is a major supplier of Soviet phosphatic fertilizers. Another is the rare igneous rock carbonatite, important as a source of niobium but also of apatite at several places in Brazil and from a huge intrusive body at Palabora in the Republic of South Africa. The major production of apatite, however, accounting for most of the

FIG. 7-5 Location of the major sites of phosphate production around the world.

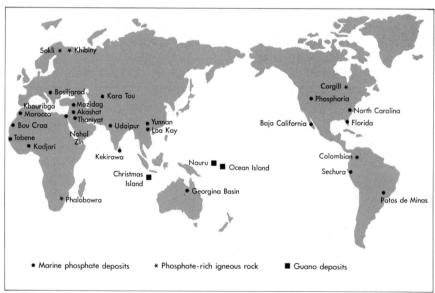

present world production and for almost all of our known reserves, is from marine sedimentary deposits. They presently supply about 82 percent of the world's phosphorus needs; the remainder comes from igneous rocks (16 percent) and from guano (2 percent) which is principally the dried manure of fish-eating seabirds.

A number of questions still surround the origin of marine phosphate deposits, but the basic pattern of formation is reasonably well understood, because the present-day deposition of apatite is an upwelling of cold, phosphorus-rich waters from the deep ocean floor. When this happens along a shallow continental shelf, as in today's sites of deposition, or in basins with restricted inflow, several effects can cause saturation of apatite to be exceeded and precipitation to ensue. For example, nearly oxygen-deficient, or anoxic, waters provide environments in which the water composition is considerably less alkaline than normal seawater and in which the solubility of apatite is exceeded. These environments are not common in the sea, especially on a large scale, and when they do form, as in basins with restricted inflow, the basin must be so situated that very little detritus is introduced to dilute the slowly precipitating apatitic sediments. In an area now in the western United States, upwelling apparently occurred (Fig. 7-6) during the Permian. The beds so formed are particularly large; they formed in a shallow marine basin covering what are now portions of the states of Idaho, Nevada, Utah, Colorado, Wyoming, and Montana (Fig. 7-7). The phosphate-rich sediments, called the Phosphoria Formation, cover more than 160,000 square kilometers and reach thicknesses of 140 meters. However, the thickness of the phosphatic bed is usually only a meter or less, and can be considered at best only a potential resource. The tonnage, though, is enormous.

Small nodular bodies of precipitated apatite are common in some limestones formed in shallow marine waters. Large concentrations of nodules, whether formed directly or concentrated secondarily into gravel beds, form valuable phosphate deposits. The huge "land pebble" phosphate deposits of Florida are the source of 85 percent of the present phosphate production in the United States; they are secondary concentrations of phosphatic nodules from Miocene limestones. Another large producing area, in Tennessee, contains residual deposits of phosphates formed by the weathering of nodule-containing limestones.

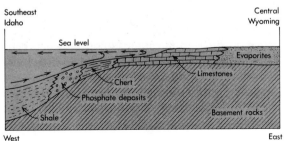

FIG. 7-6 Schematic representation of the site of apatite deposition in the Phosphoria Formation in the western U.S.A. (After R. Sheldon, 1963.)

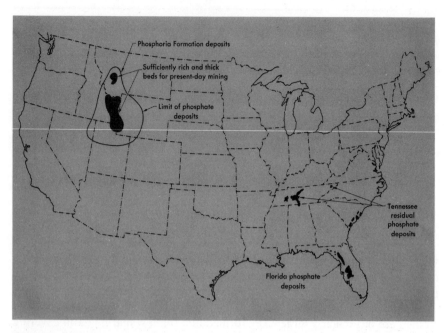

FIG. 7-7 Extensive phosphate deposits are worked in three important areas of the United States. The largest reserves are in the Phosphoria Formation and appear to be adequate for many centuries, provided that mining and transportation problems can be solved. (After V. E. McKelvey et al., 1953; Tenn. Div. of Mines, 1938; *U.S. Geol. Surv. Bull.,* 1942.)

The principal phosphate-producing countries of the world are also the principal reserve-holders, and the reserves are indeed huge—exceeding 40 billion metric tons of phosphate rock in 1982. The spotty geographic location of known resources is not encouraging, however, for transportation costs add heavily to the expense of the fertilizer. Countries such as Australia, with large land areas needing phosphatic fertilizers, have therefore actively pursued local exploration programs in the hope of finding accessible supplies. A large deposit has been located in Queensland; unfortunately, the transportation costs from this remote location to the agricultural parts of Australia have prevented exploitation.

The potential resources of phosphorus are large. Prospecting for phosphate deposits has not been thorough enough to enable certainty about whether very large deposits may still be discovered. In part this is a recognition of the economic difficulties entailed in opening new deposits in competition with existing mines. In part, too, it stems from the difficulty of recognizing phosphorus-rich rocks. Phosphate rocks look like ordinary shales and limestones even to an expert. We can, therefore, probably anticipate that additional large phosphate deposits will be discovered.

One large potential resource is already apparent. Along several continental shelves of the world there are crusts and nodules of apatite formed during the Miocene in much the same way that modern phosphate deposits are forming—these are the same formations, now uplifted onto the continent, that yield the rich phosphates in Florida and Morocco. Unfortunately, the grade of the deposits is lower than that of their landward equivalents, but the tonnages are large, probably as large as the present reserves. We must therefore conclude that the availability of phosphorus, like that of nitrogen and potassium, will not soon limit food production. It is more likely that the costs of making nitrogen salts and the costs of mining and transporting phosphorus and potassium fertilizers will be the limits to fertilizer use.

Sulfur

Sulfur has many uses and is not commonly considered a fertilizer element; approximately 40 percent of the world's production, however, is used in the manufacture of superphosphate and ammonium sulfate, both essential fertilizers. The second-largest consumer, the chemical industry, takes 20 percent and uses much of it for the production of insecticides and fungicides for crop protection.

Since sulfur is an abundant element, its sources are varied and widespread. The sea, for example, contains vast resources of *sulfate,* and the huge evaporite deposits of the world, discussed previously, contain enormous resources of $CaSO_4$. However, sulfur, like other resources, is preferentially sought in its least costly supply, which can be any of several sources depending on local circumstances. The most important in 1982, accounting for 32 percent of world production, was elemental or native sulfur.

There are two major sources of native sulfur. One source, exploited principally in Japan, and declining very rapidly in importance, is from volcanoes, which give off sulfurous gases that condense in near-surface veins and rock impregnations. The other source, quantitatively much larger, is derived by secondary concentration from $CaSO_4$. Certain anaerobic bacteria derive their oxygen from solid compounds, such as $CaSO_4$, and their food supplies from decayed organic matter. A series of reactions ensues by which the bacteria change organic compounds and $CaSO_4$ to $CaCO_3$ and S.

This process occurs where petroleum is available for bacterial food. In the United States, Mexico, and many other localities, bacterial reduction has occurred on top of salt domes and in certain evaporite beds. When salt rises from deeply buried marine evaporites, the associated $CaSO_4$ is carried with salt to a near-surface environment where sulfur is liberated by bacterial reduction. Of several hundred salt domes around the world, only a few contain commercial quantities of native sulfur. These occur principally along the coast of the Gulf of Mexico from Alabama to Mexico; they are very rich and accounted for 12 percent of the world's 1982 production. The second source is much larger but has been recognized more recently and is still a relatively small contributor to the present production. If circulating subsurface waters locally dissolve NaCl and $CaSO_4$ from an evaporite bed, petroleum and bacteria can enter the resulting voids and reduce sulfate to sulfur. This has happened on a large scale in West Texas, where more than 50×10^6 metric tons of recoverable sulfur have been found in the Culbertson Field alone. Similar large deposits are known in Iraq, Poland, and the U.S.S.R.

Compared to consumption, the reserves of native sulfur are not large, so for the last 30 years a determined drive on the part of many countries has opened three alternative sulfur sources. The first is the H_2S, or *sour gas,* content of natural gas. Formerly allowed to escape, the H_2S component is now widely recovered and oxidized to sulfur. The second source of sulfur is in the sulfide ores of the scarce metals, and in deposits of two iron sulfides, pyrite (FeS_2) and pyrrhotite (FeS), from which sulfur is recovered as a by-product. The third source of sulfur is $CaSO_4$, which is used in several European countries as new material for sulfuric acid.

The world production of sulfur from all sources reached 52,000,000 tons in 1982; of this 10,100,000 metric tons were produced by the United States. Reserves of rich native sulfur ores are relatively small, but resources of sulfide and sulfate ores are huge. Provided that technological development can keep the price of sulfur low as the alternative resources are used, we shall always have abundant supplies. One example of a technological advance can already be cited: To reduce the amount of sulfur dioxide being released to the atmosphere from coal-burning power plants, means have been developed to recover the sulfur dioxide.

MINERALS FOR CHEMICALS

The nonmetallic minerals used principally for raw materials in the chemical industry are diverse and of considerable economic importance. They have few claims to being essential compounds, however, and the uses of most are guided chiefly by their great abundance, easy recovery, and hence low cost. Substitutes are available for many.

The most important member of the group is the mineral halite (NaCl). Not only does the sea contain vast resources of salt (see Chapter 2), but marine evaporites also contain such vast quantities of NaCl that problems of resources essentially become problems of the practicality of mining and shipping (Fig. 7-4). The Permian-aged evaporite basin of the south and central United States, for example, contains more than 150,000 square kilometers of halite beds aggregating 60 meters in thickness, but the present cost of mining the deposits is high because they are relatively deep and far from major markets; they are exploited only in one small area in Kansas.

Although many beds are too deep to mine, nature has an interesting way of bringing salt nearer the surface. Halite has a density of 2.2 grams per cubic centimeter, whereas most of the associated sedimentary rocks have densities of at least 2.5 grams per cubic centimeter. The salt beds, being lighter and capable of plastic flow like ice in a glacier, tend to rise and "flow" up through the overlying rocks. If the overlying rocks are weak enough to be ruptured by the rising salt, long thin columns or plugs of salt float up from deeply buried sedimentary salt horizons. Columns ranging from about 100 meters to more than 2 kilometers in diameter are known to have risen up through as much as 12 kilometers of overlying sediments.

Salt domes are known in many areas of the world—Europe, South America, the Middle East, and the U.S.S.R.—but they are particularly frequent in the area bordering the Gulf of Mexico, where several hundred have been identified (Fig. 7-8). These domes have risen from evaporite beds 12,000 meters below the present flat coastal plain of Louisiana and Texas, and several are mined for salt.

Salt is an essential ingredient in our diets, and 99 countries produce it on a regular basis. Direct human consumption is only a small portion of the total, however, since most goes for the manufacture of chlorine and soda ash (Na_2CO_3) in the chemical industry and for road control of ice and snow. Not surprisingly, the major industrial powers—the United States, the U.S.S.R., and West Germany, together with China, home of 20 percent of the world's population, consumed 50 percent of the 1982 production of 182,000,000 metric tons.

Of the raw chemical group, with the exclusion of petrochemicals derived from fossil fuels, salt has the largest production. Others of importance are Na_2CO_3, used for production of paper, soap, and detergents, and for water treatment; Na_2SO_4, used for kraft paper, detergents, and additives in tanning and dyeing; and borate minerals such as borax ($Na_2B_4O_7 \cdot 10H_2O$), used for glass-making fluxes, soaps, detergents, hide-curing compounds, and antiseptics. These deposits are all formed by precipitation from lake waters in *nonmarine evaporite deposits,* and although many individual deposits are not very large, the deposits are widespread.

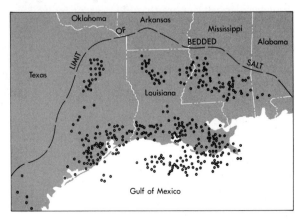

FIG. 7-8 Salt domes of the Gulf Coast region of the United States. Note that salt domes are confined to well-marked zones, even though a much larger region is underlain by the Louann salt from which the domes rise. (After D. H. Kupfer, 1970.)

OTHER INDUSTRIAL MINERALS

The list is long but only one group, the abrasive minerals, is so technologically essential that it requires discussion.

Abrasives are vitally important for working hard modern alloys and compounds such as tungsten carbide, and it is diamond, the hardest known natural compound, that is the most important resource. Diamond—the most dense natural form of carbon—requires high pressures for its formation; these are reached only at depths of 150 kilometers or more in the earth. The diamond-bearing rocks from these great depths, called *kimberlites,* come from the mantle and are themselves rare. They reach the surface in narrow pipe-like vents, often no more than 50 meters in diameter. The reasons for the formation and location of the pipes remain a geological puzzle.

Kimberlites are the home of diamonds, but not all kimberlites contain diamonds. Of the many hundreds of kimberlite pipes found in Africa to date, fewer than 40 are known to contain diamonds, and of these a third is too lean to warrant mining. On other continents the percentage is even lower, and, outside Africa, only in the Yakutia area of the U.S.S.R. and in northwestern Australia have kimberlites been discovered that are rich enough to be worked. Even the richest kimberlites contain very low diamond contents—no more than 0.0000073 percent.* Kimberlites and diamonds are found on all continents, however, and prospectors may well find new rich pipes. For example, the AK-1 pipe in northwest Australia, possibly the largest diamond-bearing pipe discovered to date, was only recognized during the 1970's. Although a number of diamonds have been discovered in the United States, most have been found in small placer deposits. A diamond-bearing kimberlite in Arkansas is more of a mineralogical curiosity than a site of potential resources. During the 1970's too, a number of small, diamond-bearing kimberlites were discovered in southern Wyoming and northern Colorado. Unfortunately the diamonds are too small and the grade too lean to warrant production.

Because diamonds are dense and almost indestructible, they accumulate in placer deposits; more than 90 percent by weight of all diamonds recovered still come from placers. We immediately think of gems when diamonds are mentioned; however, only 20 percent of the diamonds produced can be cut, although this still amounts to 65 percent or more of the monetary value of diamond production. The remaining 80 percent of all diamonds produced are used for industrial purposes such as cutting, die-making, and the manufacture of abrasives.

From the time of their discovery in 1870, African deposits have been the world's largest producers of diamonds. The first African production came from South Africa, with kimberlite pipe production rich in gem material, but

---

*This is equivalent to 0.2 gram (1 carat) for each three metric tons of rock.

Table 7-3 Production of gem and industrial diamonds during 1981. Note how widely the ratio of gem to industrial diamonds varies from country to country.

Country	DIAMOND PRODUCTION (MILLIONS OF GRAMS)		
	Gemstones	Industrial	Total
U.S.S.R.	0.42	1.70	2.12
Rep. of South Africa	0.69	1.22	1.91
Zaire	0.05	1.45	1.50
Botswana	0.15	0.84	0.99
Namibia	0.24	0.01	0.25
World Total	2.02	5.80	7.82

(After U.S. Bureau of Mines).

more recently pipe deposits in Tanzania, Lesotho, and Botswana have been discovered, and production has been developed from placers in Zaire and Namibia. The African deposits have produced over 80 percent of the world's diamonds (Table 7-3). Production in northern Siberia accounts for the growing Soviet production. During the last 25 years, more than 400 kimberlite pipes have been discovered in a region measuring about 400 by 500 kilometers located southwest of the Lena River. It is probable that many more will be found.

Both measured reserves and probable resources of gem and industrial diamonds are large but it is almost impossible to give a meaningful figure. Technological progress has finally shown the way to self-sufficiency where industrial diamonds are concerned. In 1955, the General Electric Company announced its successful synthesis of industrial diamonds, using a special ultra-high-pressure reaction vessel. By 1981 commercial production of diamonds had grown to 11,400,000 grams per year in the United States alone; additional large production is coming from Sweden, South Africa, Ireland, Japan, and the U.S.S.R.

eight

building materials

There will be a shortage of standing room on earth before there is a shortage of granite. (J.A.S. Adams, New Ways of Finding Minerals, 1959.)

Building materials are the largest crop and, after fossil fuels, the second most valuable group of mineral commodities that we reap from the earth. Because almost every known rock type and mineral contributes to the crop in some way, discussion of the origin of building materials embraces most of geology, and that is beyond the scope of this book. This chapter will therefore concentrate mainly on the uses of building materials in order to try to place these largest-volume mineral products into perspective with the other mineral products.

Although no classification is completely satisfactory, we will separate building materials into the following two groups: first, materials that are used as they come from the ground, without any treatment beyond physical shaping, such as cutting or crushing; second, the prepared materials that must be chemically treated, fired, melted, or otherwise altered before use. Treatment is needed so that the materials can be molded and shaped into new forms. The first group includes building stones, sand, gravel, and crushed stone for aggregate; the second includes clay for bricks, raw materials for cement, plaster, and asbestos.

Many building materials, unlike metals, have little intrinsic value; they are not scarce commodities and they are widely distributed, but when removed and processed to a useful form, their value increases enormously. For example, the limestone and shale used to make cement may have intrinsic values of less than $1 per metric ton in the ground, but after mining, crushing, firing, and conversion to a high-quality cement, the product is worth $50 or more per ton (Fig. 8-1). The factors controlling the location of production sites are commonly those of local demand and of transportation costs; rarely are there problems of resource abundance.

NATURAL ROCK PRODUCTS

There are three important classes of natural rock products; the supplies of each are almost limitless, and it makes little sense to consider global reserves.

Building Stone

The uses of building stones range from roofing slate and curbstones to facings for public buildings and tombstones. Though used from time immemorial as structural and foundation materials, building stone is being supplanted by concrete; its remaining uses are largely governed by the pleasing ornamental display of natural stone. In buildings, for example, it is used largely as a facing material. Not surprisingly, the production of shaped building stone has been declining for many years.

Figures for the production volume and types of stone used are not available on a worldwide basis; however, the best-documented production—that from the United States—probably gives a reasonable idea of the kinds of rocks used around the world. The total tonnage of building stones mined in the United States was 1.2 million metric tons in 1982. The two most popular rock

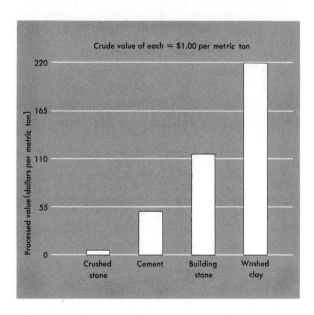

FIG. 8-1 Processing of building materials adds greatly to their value.

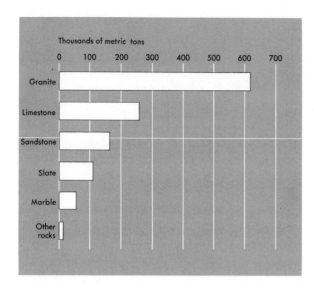

FIG. 8-2 Types of building stones used in the United States during 1981. Although direct figures are unavailable, it is probable that the same approximate range of rock types is used throughout the world. (After U.S. Bureau of Mines.)

types were limestone and granite, which together accounted for more than 70 percent of the total production (Fig. 8-2).

What problems are encountered with production of building stones? When stones of pleasing appearance and good physical properties are located, problems have mostly to do with quarrying—how to quarry the rock without shattering it, which means that extensive blasting is not possible, and how to select areas where natural joints and cracks in rocks are a help, rather than a hindrance, to mining.

Crushed Rock

A commodity of enormous proportions, crushed rock accounted for 800 million metric tons in 1982 in the United States alone, the figure for the world being more than 2.5 billion metric tons. Yet little more than a century has passed since Eli Whitney Blake, moved by the difficulty of preparing by hand the quantities of crushed rock needed for the then ambitious project of a 2-mile long macadam road from New Haven to Westville, Connecticut, invented the modern rock crusher in 1858. Until that date, all rock crushing was done by hand.

Crushed stone is still used principally for roadbeds and for concrete aggregate, although about 14 percent, principally limestone, is used as raw material for the manufacture of cement. The most widely used rock types are limestone and dolostone, both easy to mine and crush, but strong in use. Basalt and other fine-grained, dark-colored igneous rocks, commonly called *trap rock* by industry, are a poor second (Fig. 8-3). The only essential requirement for crushed stone is a rock outcrop to quarry; rock crushers can be seen—and heard—adjacent to most cities around the world.

FIG. 8-3 Rock types most widely used during 1981 in the preparation of crushed stone in the United States. (After U.S. Bureau of Mines.)

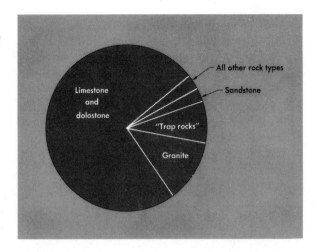

Sand and Gravel

Sand and gravel, largely used like crushed rock for highway roadbeds and for concrete aggregate, are consumed in amounts even larger than those of crushed stone. The combined consumption in the United States in 1982 was 835 million metric tons. Sand is comprised of mineral particles that are less than 2 millimeters in diameter; particles in gravel are larger. The tonnage of gravel used is twice that of sand.

Streams are the geological domain of sand and gravel. Rounded grains are produced by continuous movement of fast water, and a size separation occurs on the basis of weight: Finer grains are washed downstream or out to sea. Local resources of sand and gravel may often be limited, especially in flat regions and in places devoid of large rivers. Where land resources are being depleted too rapidly, exploration and exploitation of offshore marine sandbars may also be employed. An interesting situation has now been reached in both Europe and North America: Population densities in coastal areas above about 40 degrees north latitude have consumed much of the available sand and gravel. It is precisely in these high latitudes, however, that extensive sand and gravel deposits occur on the continental margins, having been deposited there by glaciers during the height of the recent ice age. These communities therefore can either quarry and crush rock or dredge sand and gravel from beneath the sea. Hundreds of millions of dollars worth of sand and gravel are now dredged each year off the west coast of Europe. In North America dredging has commenced in a small way, and it can be expected to grow in the years ahead, particularly off the shores of New Jersey, New York, and the New England states.

Gravel deposits are sparse or absent off many tropical coasts. Around the Gulf of Mexico, for example, sands can be found in river deltas, but gravels are nearly unknown. In the Gulf Coast area igneous and metamorphic rock do not reach the surface, so hard rock is not available for crushing. The only coarse building materials under the circumstances are old shell beds, particularly oyster shells, clam shells, and coral reefs. As the limited supplies of these materials are used up, areas such as southern Texas, Louisiana, and Florida are forced to import gravel or crushed stone.

PREPARED ROCK PRODUCTS

We have been using prepared rock products since the day someone first modeled a clay object and fired it in a hearth. Although we now process and use a bewilderingly large array of materials, five of these account for most of the volume and value.

Cement

The word *cement* refers to agents that bind particles together. Cement is not used alone; it is added to sand, gravel, crushed rock, oyster shells, or other aggregate as the binder needed to make mortar or concrete, a sort of "instant rock." As little as 15 percent of a concrete may be cement.

The forerunner of modern cement was discovered by the engineers of ancient Rome. They found that water added to a mixture of quicklime (CaO, obtained by heating—or calcining—limestone) and a natural, glassy volcanic ash from the town of Pozzuoli, near Naples, produced a series of reactions that caused the mixture to recrystallize and harden. The resulting mass was stable in air or water. The Romans used the cement, known as *pozzolan cement,* in many of their remarkable engineering feats. Similar materials are still employed today, but only on a small scale. In a pozzolan cement one of the ingredients (quicklime) is calcined to get it in a reactive form; the other ingredient, volcanic ash, is naturally reactive. However, volcanic ash has also been essentially calcined by nature during the volcanic eruption; it was not long before some asked whether all the ingredients could be calcined if the right rock compositions were selected. When the Romans answered the question, they discovered the secret of cement manufacture.

The "secret" was forgotten during the Dark Ages and was rediscovered in 1756. John Smeaton, a British engineer engaged in designing and building the famous Eddystone Lighthouse, sought cementing materials that would set and remain stable under seawater. He is said to have rediscovered the Roman cement formula while reading Latin documents. Cements soon became popular in Europe and were subject to much experimentation. In 1824 another Englishman, Joseph Aspidin, patented his formula for *portland cement,* so called because its color resembled Portland stone, a limestone widely used in British buildings. Portland cement soon supplanted all other cements and is today the most common construction material in the world. Twice as much concrete is now used as all other structural materials combined.

Production of portland cement has grown erratically but continuously as populations have grown and technological expansions have occurred around the world; the growth is expected to continue, especially in parts of the world where living standards are rising most rapidly. Not surprisingly, the largest producers and consumers are the highly industrialized countries (Table 8-1).

Table 8-1 Producers of cement, 1982.

Country*	Production (metric tons)	Percentage of Total
U.S.S.R.	127×10^6	14.3
China	86×10^6	9.7
Japan	85×10^6	9.6
U.S.A.	58×10^6	6.5
Italy	41×10^6	5.6
West Germany	33×10^6	3.7
France	27×10^6	3.1
World Total	889×10^6	100

*Production was reported from 117 countries, 10 more than a decade earlier, and percentage of world production changed markedly in the same period, with declines in the U.S.S.R. and the United States, but increases in Japan and China. For many countries, production capacity is considerably larger than actual production.

(After U.S. Bureau of Mines).

Portland cements have a wide range of composition depending on their use and are prepared by heating ground rock of suitable composition to a temperature of approximately 1,480°C. Heating expels all the carbon dioxide and water and causes part of the charge to melt to a glass. The resulting clinker is crushed to a powder and is then ready for use; when the powder is mixed with water, a series of chemical reactions proceed in which new compounds form and grow into a hard cemented mass of interlocking crystals.

The raw materials for portland cement (Fig. 8-4) are found in a suitable mixture of dolostone or limestone (or slightly dolomitic limestone) plus shale or clay. Since limestone is the largest ingredient, cement works are usually situated close to a suitable source of limestone; the other ingredients are transported in. The most desirable new material is a somewhat impure limestone in which the impurities are clays of the desired composition. Such beds are indeed found, and natural cement rocks now account for approximately 20 percent of the cement production.

Plaster

Plaster, made by heating or calcinating gypsum ($CaSO_4 \cdot 2H_2O$), is one of our oldest building materials. The worldwide production was 75 million metric tons in 1982 and is continuing to grow. Calcining gypsum at 177°C rapidly drives off 75 percent of the water and changes the gypsum to a new compound, $2CaSO_4 \cdot H_2O$, that is commonly called *plaster of Paris* after the

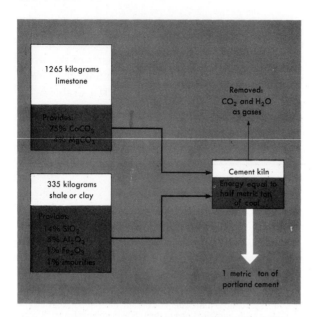

FIG. 8-4 Typical mix of raw materials needed to produce a widely used composition of portland cement.

famous gypsum quarries in the northern part of that city, from which a plaster of particularly high quality is produced. When plaster of Paris is mixed with water, it reverts to a finely interlocked mass of tiny gypsum crystals. Plaster can be used alone, mixed with sand, or mounted on wallboard or paper backings for prefabricated finished surfaces. It has many other uses too. Approximately 20 percent is used agriculturally for addition to soil to neutralize alkalinity, and a significant fraction is added to cement to slow down the setting process.

In Chapter 7 the precipitation of $CaSO_4$ in evaporite sequences was discussed. The precipitation may take one of two forms, either gypsum or anhydrite ($CaSO_4$), so named because it does not contain any water of crystallization. Which of the two forms precipitates is a function of temperature. Anhydrite is favored at higher temperatures; in the hot climates where most evaporites form, anhydrite is a common mineral. Anhydrite tends to hydrate to gypsum in the same way that plaster of Paris does, and much material that was originally anhydrite is mined as gypsum today.

Gypsum and anhydrite are widely distributed; more common than salt but less common than limestone, they are known throughout the Phanerozoic geologic record. A resource map published by the U.S. Geological Survey shows that as much as 10 percent of the entire land area in the United States is underlain by gypsiferous rocks; this indicates that potential resources are extremely abundant. Indeed, the U.S. Bureau of Mines has stated that reserves in the United States alone are sufficient for 2,000 years at projected rates of production.

Clays

There are many structural and refractory ceramic materials now used, and discussion of each would be pointless. Most are formed from clay that can be molded into desired shapes, then fired to hardness. Bricks so formed have been used at least since the days of the Babylonian Empire. The earliest bricks were not particularly durable because they were only allowed to dry in the sun; later, though, especially during the great middle years of the Roman Empire nearly 2,000 years ago, greater durability was achieved by kiln firing and glaze-coating. Much of the art of brickmaking was lost in Europe during the Dark Ages. From the time of the revival of an industry producing fired bricks in Europe in the thirteenth century, production of clay for structural ceramics has grown steadily—first for the preparation of bricks, and later for the production of tiles, drainpipes, and numerous other uses. By 1982, the production of clay alone was 35 million metric tons. 65 percent of this was used for structural ceramics, such as bricks, sewer pipes, tiles, and special cements. Much of the remainder was used in the manufacture of high-quality ceramics, light-weight concrete aggregate, fillers for paper, plastics, rubber, and paint, as absorbants in animal litter and oil cleaning, in oil well drilling muds, and in pottery.

Clays are formed by weathering processes at the earth's surface and may accumulate as residual deposits, as has been discussed in the section on aluminum (Chapter 5); they also may be transported and deposited as sedimentary clay beds. Whether transported or residual, clays soon begin to lithify and to become solid rocks when they are dehydrated and heated by burial. Their environment is the earth's surface and not the deeper portions of the crust. Like the other building resource materials, therefore, they are usually recovered from surficial deposits in large quarrying operations that tend to be situated close to major consuming sites.

Reserves of clays are so large that few countries make attempts to estimate them. In the United States, for example, reserves alone are said by the U.S. Bureau of Mines to be more than sufficient for another century of production at anticipated rates of growth. Potential resources are vastly larger.

Glass

We might not immediately think of glass as belonging in a category with bricks and cement, but it consumes similar raw materials and is processed in a similar fashion. Furthermore, glass has now challenged many older, more established structural materials in certain specialized uses, and consumption is rising rapidly.

Glass is made by melting rocks and minerals, then quenching them so rapidly that crystals do not have time to nucleate. This procedure is more readily carried out with some materials than with others, and most readily with silica (SiO_2), usually obtained from quartz in sandstones. The melting point of quartz is very high ($1,713°C$), so to reduce the melting temperature, ingredients such as CaO (from limestone), Na_2O (from sodium carbonate), and borax are added.

Asbestos

Asbestos is the name given to the fibrous forms of many minerals. One such, chrysotile ($Mg_3Si_2O_5[OH]_2$), a fibrous form of the serpentine minerals, is quite abundant and has such excellent physical properties that it accounts for more than 90 percent of all the asbestos mined. Other minerals used because of their asbestiform properties are crocidolite ($Na_2Fe_5Si_8O_{22}[OH]_2$) and amosite ($[Mg, Fe]_7Si_8O_{22}[OH]_2$) both produced mainly in the Republic of South Africa. Asbestos fibers are strong and flexible, and can be spun and woven like organic fibers such as cotton and wool. The resulting products are not flammable, are good electrical and thermal insulators, have excellent wear-resistant properties, and are stable in many corrosive environments. Asbestos fibers are also used to make strong, corrosion-resistant pipes by combining them with cement, floor and roofing tiles, gaskets, brake linings, and other specialized products. Fibers measuring more than a centimeter in length are preferred for making thread, and these fibers are used for electrical insulation and for other specialized uses. Short fibers are bound together by inert media, such as portland cement (to produce pipe, roof, and wall shingles) and vinyl plastics (to produce tiles).

Large deposits of chrysotile asbestos apparently form in only one way; by the near-surface hydration and alteration of the minerals in peridotite. The world's largest producer, the U.S.S.R., obtains its supplies from such a source, as does Canada, the second largest (but much smaller) producer, which recovers most of its chrysotile from a belt of altered peridotite running north-easterly across Quebec and extending into Vermont where there was formerly a small United States production. Although serpentines are not particularly uncommon rocks in mountain belts, asbestos resembles the scarce metals in its supplies, for only a tiny fraction of the serpentines have large, commercially exploitable deposits. Crocidolite, or blue asbestos, occurs as a product of low-grade metamorphism in Lake Superior-type banded iron formations. The world's largest reserves of asbestos are in the hands of the two largest producing countries, the U.S.S.R. and Canada (Table 8-2).

Recent years have been witness to a sharp decline in production and use of asbestiform minerals because of a perceived cancer hazard. Whether this perception is correct for all or just some of the mineral varieties, and for all or just certain fiber sizes remains to be demonstrated, but until necessary tests have been made it is not likely that asbestos mining will be a very healthy industry.

Table 8-2 Producers of asbestos minerals in 1981, mainly chrysotile.*

Country	Production (metric tons)
U.S.S.R.	2.22×10^6
Canada	1.13×10^6
China	0.25×10^6
Zimbabwe	0.25×10^6
Rep. So. Africa[†]	0.24×10^6
Brazil	0.18×10^6
World Total	4.73×10^6

*Reserves are large, reportedly in excess of 100×10^6 metric tons.
[†]A large fraction is crocidolite.

NONMETALLICS IN THE FUTURE

The future seems bright for most nonmetallic minerals. Reserves tend to be large and potential resources even larger. Some commodities such as building stone are so abundant that it is pointless to even attempt to put numbers on reserves. Viewing the resource abundance, some experts have suggested that nonmetallic minerals should be considered similar to abundant metals, and that society should try to find ways to use nonmetallics to replace scarce metals and other commodities in short supply. Perhaps this will be possible, because glass fibers are already being used in some places to transmit telephone messages. If replacement of metals by nonmetals became widespread, the resultant society might look rather different from today's society. The nonmetals seem to provide yet another example of abundant and underused resources awaiting innovative technological advances through research in the area of material sciences.

nine

water

. . . pure water is becoming a critical commodity whose abundance is about to set an upper limit of economic evolution in a few parts of the Nation and inevitably will do so rather widely within half a century or less. Prudence requires that the Nation learn to manage water supplies boldly, imaginatively, and with utmost efficiency. Time in which to develop such competence is all too short. (A. M. Piper, U.S. Geological Survey, Water-Supply Paper #1797, 1965.)

Water is such a vital resource that to attempt to assign it a cash value would be pointless; simply put, it is the most valuable of all our resources. To survive, human beings require at least 1.4 liters of water a day; our bodies are about 70 percent water by weight. Soils require water to support plant life. Without a hydrosphere there could be no life on earth.

Although much water is locked in the minerals of the crust, it is the free water of the hydrosphere from which we must draw our resources. The total amount of water in the hydrosphere is estimated to be 1.36×10^9 cubic kilometers, or 1.35×10^{21} liters, but it is very unevenly distributed (Fig. 9-1), with 97.2 percent residing in the oceans and another 2.15 percent trapped in the polar icecaps and glaciers. The remaining 0.65 percent of the water in the hydrosphere is the fraction on which we now rely, and it would soon be consumed were it not for the well-known hydrological cycle (Fig. 9-2). The cycle of evaporation by solar heat plus transpiration, followed by condensation and precipitation, assures a continuous supply and makes water a renewable resource. Questions concerning water therefore have less to do with total abundance than with local distribution and local rates of use. Some areas are well supplied; others are water poor. More than any other factor, availability of water determines the ultimate population capacity of a geographic province.

	Location	Water volume (liters)	Percentage of total water
Surface water			
	Fresh-water lakes	125×10^{15}	.009
	Saline lakes and inland seas	104×10^{15}	.008
	Average in stream channels	1×10^{15}	.0001
Subsurface water			
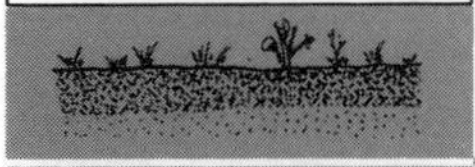	Vadose water (includes soil moisture)	67×10^{15}	.005
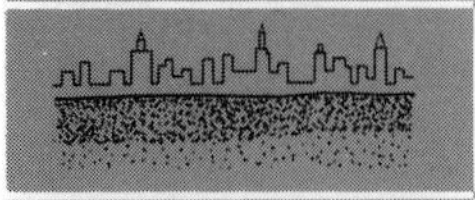	Ground water within depth of half a mile	$4,170 \times 10^{15}$	.31
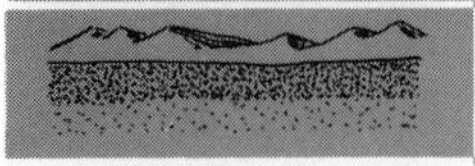	Ground water—deep lying	$4,170 \times 10^{15}$	.31
Other water locations			
	Icecaps and glaciers	$29,000 \times 10^{15}$	2.15
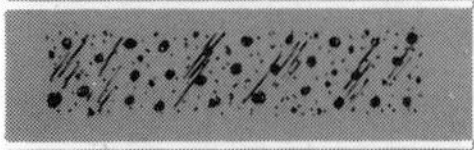	Atmosphere	13×10^{15}	.001
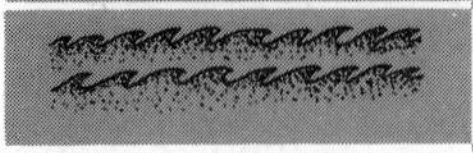	World ocean	$1,320,000 \times 10^{15}$	97.2

FIG. 9-1 Distribution of water in the hydrosphere. (After U.S. Geological Survey.)

DISTRIBUTION OF PRECIPITATED WATER

Precipitation is distributed very unevenly around the world. A belt of high rainfall straddles the equator and is flanked by two desert, or low-precipitation, belts (Fig. 9-3). In the United States, where much information is available on the details of the hydrological cycle, an average of 5.88×10^{15} liters of water falls as rain and snow each year. The rainfall is very uneven; precipitation varies by a factor of 20 or more across large provinces (Fig. 9-3). The regional disparities that develop as a result of this are perhaps best demonstrated by the fact that the area east of the Mississippi River receives 65 percent of the country's total rainfall (excluding Alaska and Hawaii), whereas the area west of the Mississippi receives only 35 percent.

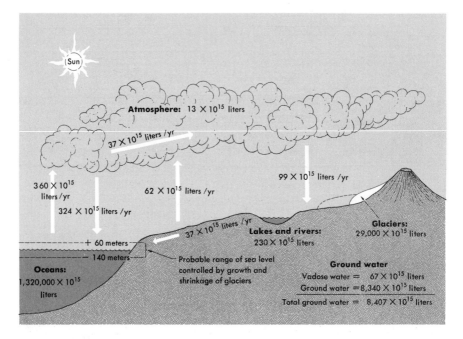

FIG. 9-2 The hydrosphere and the hydrologic cycle. (After A. L. Bloom, *The Surface of the Earth,* Prentice-Hall, 1969.)

In addition to geographic variations, there are marked temporal variations in precipitation. Seasonal variations are, of course, obvious to all, but there are also large fluctuations in precipitation related to long-term, and thus far unexplained, weather cycles (Fig. 9-4). Although water is a renewable resource, the rate of renewal clearly is neither constant nor uniform around the world. Effective use of available water, therefore, requires both storage systems and efficient means by which to distribute water to places of major consumption. Storage dams and distribution systems both use mineral resources—for cements, pipes, pumps, and valves—and provide a striking example of the many ways that use of one resource depends on the availability of other resources.

EVAPORATION AND TRANSPIRATION

Water will *evaporate* from any wetted surface; a significant fraction of the rainfall that falls on land is returned to the atmosphere in this fashion. In addition, water is assimilated by the root systems of growing plants, pumped up stems and limbs as sap, and then *transpired* from the leaf surfaces by a process essentially identical to evaporation. The two effects, evaporation and transpiration, cannot be individually discriminated for their effectiveness in returning rainfall to the atmosphere, but their sum contribution can be evaluated and is usually called the *evapotranspiration* factor. The fraction of rain

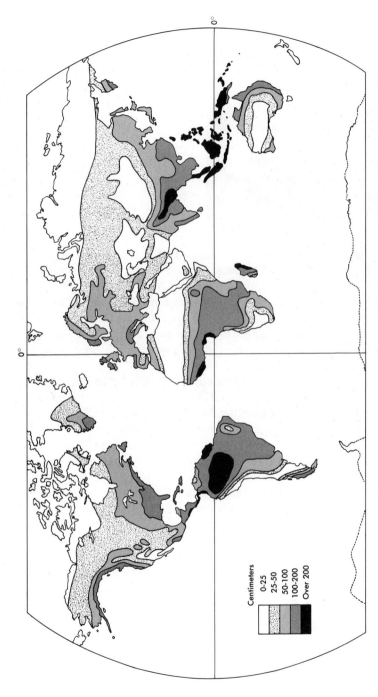

FIG. 9-3 Average precipitation around the world. Note that the eastern half of North America enjoys a plentiful rainfall, while the western half is relatively dry.

Centimeters

0-25
25-50
50-100
100-200
Over 200

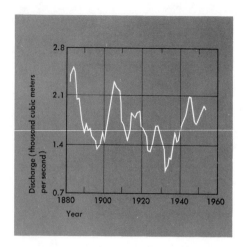

FIG. 9-4 Variations in the water discharge of the Mississippi River at Keokuk, Iowa, reflecting unexplained long-term variations in the rainfall and climate of the Mississippi River's drainage basin. (After U.S. Geological Survey.)

falling on the United States that is returned to the atmosphere by evapotranspiration, for example, is 70 percent; for the world, it is approximately 62 percent (see Fig. 9-2). In arid countries, such as Australia, the fraction is larger, and in less arid areas, such as the United Kingdom, it is lower. Water returned to the atmosphere by evapotranspiration is unavailable except in the sense that useful plants can be grown in place of useless ones. It cannot be easily trapped and redistributed for industrial or other purposes until it once again falls as rain.

In regions of low rainfall, plant cover will develop to the point that all precipitation is used in evapotranspiration and none remains for stream flow. Seasonal rainfall provides a qualifier for this statement, because streams are apt to flow even in the most arid areas during periods of very high rainfall. In general, if the evapotranspiration that results from a maximum plant cover exceeds precipitation, stream flow ceases. Conversely, if evapotranspiration is less than precipitation, streams flow.

The amount of water by which precipitation exceeds evapotranspiration is the perennial yield of stream flow water, and this is referred to as the usable fraction of rain and snowfall. The usable fraction is that portion of the rainfall that is available for storage, distribution, and other human-directed activities. Across the entire United States the usable fraction amounts to 30 percent of the total rainfall, or approximately 1.77×10^{15} liters per year. Essentially the entire eastern half of the United States, together with a small region in the Pacific northwest, enjoys a water surplus, while most of the country to the west of the Mississippi is water deficient; much of it is semiarid or arid.

GROUND WATER

Although rainfall is the only water supply available on a long-term basis, there is also a very important temporary reservoir. Water in any form that occurs in the ground is commonly called *subsurface water*. It is one of our most important water resources, but unfortunately its rate of replenishment is often so slow that overly rapid withdrawal can cause serious local ground water depletion. Indeed, in some areas the rate of renewal is so slow that subsurface water has to be considered a nonrenewable resource. Subsurface water is commonly divided into three interrelated water masses—ground water, vadose water, and soil water. Beneath the land areas of the world there is a zone where all rock pores and openings are saturated with water. This is *ground water,* and the upper surface of the saturated zone is the *water table.* The water table may lie at the surface, as in a lake or stream, or hundreds of meters below the surface; however, it is almost always present. Water below the water table moves by seepage and flows slowly to the seas or to the interior basins (see Fig. 9-2). Ground water can thus be considered analogous to a large, very slow river. The residence time of ground water, defined as the time required to reach the sea, ranges from days to hundreds of thousands of years. The water table is not horizontal; because of the varying degrees of resistance offered by rocks to the flow of ground water, it tends to be irregular and to reflect the topography above it (Fig. 9-5).

Above the water table there is an unsaturated region of *vadose water.* The region of *soil water* lies near the surface, where plant roots are abundant. Soil water moves neither up nor down, but adheres to the surface of mineral grains. Somewhat deeper, but still in the unsaturated zone, vadose water seeps slowly down to join the body of ground water below. Vadose waters cannot be considered direct resources as can ground waters, but it is the vadose waters that serve to replenish—albeit slowly—water withdrawn from the ground water zone.

The amount of ground water is huge (Fig. 9-1), an estimated 3,000 times larger than the volume of water in all the rivers at any given time. The major problems in its exploitation are threefold. First, where rock porosity is very low and permeability poor, flow into wells is exceedingly slow and water can only be removed at a very slow rate. Adequate recovery thus requires a suitably porous and permeable aquifer as a supplier. Second, the rate of replenishment is slow because much of the supply—rainfall—runs off in rivers. It has been estimated, for example, that it would take about 150 years to recharge the ground water resources in the United States to a depth of 750 meters if all the water that is now there were removed. The recharge of some areas

FIG. 9-5   Relation between subsurface waters, water table, and topography.

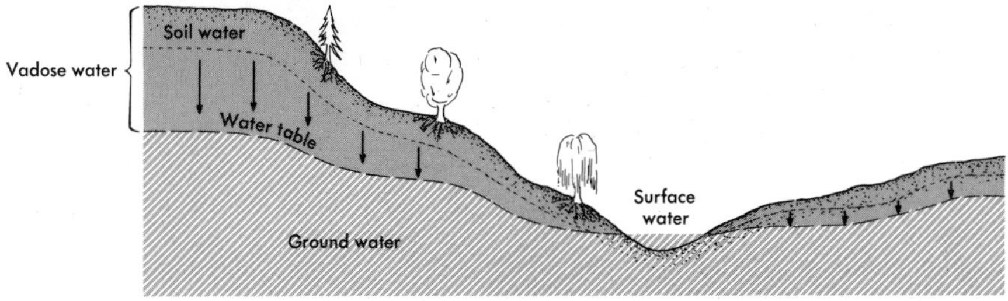

would, of course, be slower than others. The question of recharge rate for
ground water is of considerable importance, because approximately 70 percent
of all water used in the United States today is pumped subsurface water. This
is true even in the well-watered areas of the eastern part of the country. Many
municipal water supplies pump subsurface water into temporary surface reservoirs prior to distribution. If water is pumped from the ground at a rate
greater than the rate of replenishment, ground water is essentially being mined.
This is now an acute problem in parts of the arid southwestern United States,
where water has been withdrawn, largely for irrigation, at rates of up to 100
times greater than those of replenishment. If all pumping were to cease, it
would take periods of up to 100 years or more before replenishment was complete. Similar problems, sometimes with even larger replenishment periods,
are being encountered in many arid parts of the world.

Finally, there is the problem of the quality of ground water. As water
moves through rocks, it dissolves the more soluble constituents. The amount
of dissolution varies with host rock, water depth, flow rates, and other factors.
In general, water containing more than 0.05 percent (500 parts per million)
dissolved salts is unsuitable for human consumption; water with more than
0.2 percent dissolved salts is unsuitable for most other uses. However, waters
as saline as 1 percent can be used for some special purposes. The portion of
the United States underlain by rocks that are porous and permeable enough
to serve as aquifers that will yield good-quality water into wells at flow rates
of 190 liters per minute or more is extensive (Fig. 9-6), and wise development

FIG. 9-6 Regions of the United States underlain by aquifers capable of yielding water
containing 0.2 percent dissolved solids or less at rates of 190 liters per minute from individual wells. (After H. E. Thomas, 1955.)

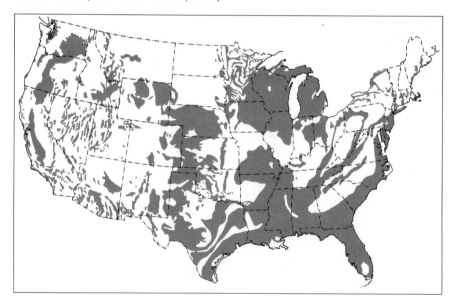

and utilization of these resources is now the prime concern of many able scientists and engineers.

RATES OF USE AND RESERVES

In 1965 a water specialist for the U.S. Department of the Interior cogently stated that " . . . all parts of the [United States] either have or will have water problems. The well-watered Eastern and Southern States are beginning to share a concern about water that has been felt in the arid West since its settlement. As industrial development and urbanization expand in the East, it is becoming more apparent each year that lack of water may deter growth unless action is taken to assure a continued supply." It is increasingly evident that the statement is correct. Similar kinds of statements can be made for many parts of the world. Towns and cities once thought immune to water shortage problems, such as the towns of Connecticut, have recently had to live with temporary water restrictions.

The current use of rainfall across the United States is summarized in Fig. 9-7. Approximately 8 percent of the rain falling in the United States, amounting to 0.42×10^{15} liters, is withdrawn for use in the categories shown. Of course, not all of the water withdrawn for use is consumed in a single use cycle. Water used to cool industrial machines, for example, can be returned to streams and reused. Irrigation and other agricultural water, however, is very

FIG. 9-7 General distribution and use of the annual precipitation in the United States. (After A. Wolman, Water Resources, Pub. 1000-B, Committee on Natural Resources, National Academy of Sciences, National Research Council, Washington, D.C., 1962.)

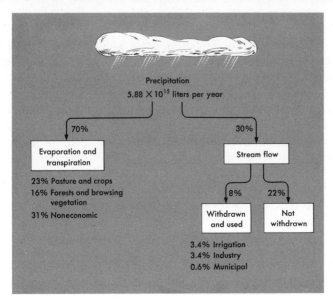

largely consumed by evapotranspiration and hence is lost; it has been estimated that 25 percent of all water now used in the United States is so consumed and thus is unavailable for further use.

Taking account of the fraction of water consumed, and projecting future population growth, it has been estimated that by the year 2000 the use of water in the United States may rise to a volume equivalent to 81 percent of the stream flow. Much of the water will be withdrawn from ground water, but it is apparent, nevertheless, that wise management and multiple use of water resources must be practiced where possible.

Stream flow varies with time, but our water demands rarely coincide with the flow cycle. We are forced to build suitable damming, storage, and reticulation schemes so that excess flows during good seasons can be conserved to supplement diminished flows during poor seasons. In so doing, of course, large open reservoirs and lakes are created and evaporation loss inevitably rises. Though experts differ, it has been optimistically stated that as much as 90 percent of the stream flow water could eventually be utilized. Even this optimistic estimate, which is made under the assumption that the necessary engineering and political problems could all be overcome, is dangerously close to the predicted withdrawal needs by the year 2000. The sense of urgency expressed by Dr. Piper is very real.

Rainfall, stream flow, and ground water are reserves. The oceans and the polar icecaps are potential resources, but both present use problems of vast magnitude. Seawater must be desalinated (in other words, rid of its salts), and polar ice, though fresh water, has to somehow be brought to consumption areas. Many desalination plants working on distillation principles are already in operation, but the cost of such plants and the power to drive them make desalinated water expensive—about 20 to 40 cents per 1,000 liters, which is at least 10 times more expensive than water from even the most expensive dam and reservoir system used for irrigation. Fresh water produced by desalination costs about the same as water delivered to our houses by municipal water schemes. Use of polar ice has not yet been tried. One study in the 1960's suggested that a tugboat could pull an iceberg 250 meters thick by 3,000 meters long by 3,000 meters wide from Antarctica to the arid west coast of Australia for about \$1 million. If the iceberg could be encased in a plastic sheet to prevent melting and mixing with seawater, 790×10^9 liters of water could be delivered for a cost within a competitive range for economic use as irrigation water.

One problem with the use and reuse of water does not afflict other resources—the problem of pollution. All the projections and discussions made for water use are made under the assumption that adequate water purity is maintained. The seriousness of the problem of water pollution is self-evident. As the percentage of stream flow withdrawn for use rises, it becomes less and less feasible to use the same stream channels for effluent disposal; a small quantity of polluted water can cause a whole stream to become polluted and hence unusable. The world's growing population is producing a water supply problem fast enough; to compound the problem by failure to control pollution, and hence to squander our most valuable natural resource, would be foolhardy in the extreme. Yet we are clearly not listening to the advice of knowledgeable experts. Today, more than one billion people in the world regularly drink unsanitary polluted water, and at least 500 million of them are continually sick as a result. Not surprisingly, the death rate due to polluted water is estimated to be in excess of 10 million people a year. Many of today's water problems are particularly serious in technologically undeveloped countries, but the problems are spreading and will continue to spread unless very careful management is exercised.

epilogue

We fool ourselves if we try to view the use of any natural resource—whether renewable or nonrenewable—as if the use can somehow be isolated from all other resources. Our patterns of use for earth's resources are interrelated in so many complex ways that the use of each commodity influences to some extent the use of every other resource. Use patterns have developed the way they have through a combination of technological advances, economic opportunity, and social acceptance. Changes will undoubtedly occur in the future in response to new technological and economic opportunities.

No one can predict exactly how technology and the economic climate will change, however, so changes in use patterns of resources cannot be exactly predicted either. Some mineral resources may become very expensive because supplies are limited and substitutes cannot take their places; other resources may become abundant and inexpensive because an unforeseen technological discovery turns a presently uneconomic potential resource into a rich ore. Interaction among technological ingenuity, economic opportunism, and the many natural resources available makes for a very flexible system. Just how flexible the system of resource usage really is, is something we will learn in the future. The conclusions drawn in Chapter 6 concerning the limited availability of geochemically scarce metals suggest that it is this group of resources that may pose the first serious test to the flexibility of the system.

There is another vital aspect to use of natural resources, however—the changes that our use patterns wreak on the local and global environment. We cannot burn fossil fuels without adding to the atmosphere at least some of the ingredients that produce acid rains. We may reduce the amounts of unpleasant ingredients released but we cannot eliminate them entirely. Nor can we burn fossil fuels without adding carbon dioxide to the atmosphere at a faster rate than that at which natural processes can remove the gas if we are to keep the composition of the atmosphere in balance. When the world's population was small and per capita consumption rates of natural resources were a small fraction of today's rates, environmental changes such as air and water pollution were local problems. Now the effects are worldwide. As use rates of natural resources continue to increase, so too will we increase the rate at which we are changing the global environment. Inevitably, therefore, responses to growing environmental concerns have become a factor to be considered in the way we use resources. Safe burial of nuclear waste is an example of the way such an interaction can occur; until a completely safe and acceptable way to dispose of nuclear wastes is developed, we cannot reasonably consider development of an extensive system of nuclear power plants.

It is my suspicion that one to two centuries hence, society will probably develop a living pattern in which most people will live in cities with very high population densities—many times more dense than population densities of most cities today—so that land suitable for agriculture can be used for food production. The main source of energy will be the sun, and although I do not know how we will convert solar energy to electricity, I suspect that electricity will be the way in which energy will be distributed and used. The minerals used by this future society will be largely the geochemically abundant metals, iron and aluminum, together with abundant nonmetallic materials, especially glass. The geochemically scarce metals will still be used, but per capita consumptions will decline to a tiny fraction of today's values because the costs of all the metals, including such common ones as copper, lead, and zinc, will have risen to levels such that it will not be possible to use the metals for most purposes of building or transportation. Material and energy uses will, in effect, be freed from supply restraints.

The problems of environmental changes will probably not have been solved a century ahead. Indeed, they may have become much worse. I make this gloomy suggestion because I suspect that the population will grow and will be much larger than it is today. It does not seem likely, or even possible, for many billions of people to live on a small planet like the earth without causing major changes in the environment.

How the global society will reach a stable size and a state in which everyone has equal access to resources I cannot foresee. What is possible to predict, however, is that the period of greatest challenge so far as development of resources and changes in the environment are concerned has already commenced and will continue for the next 50 to 100 years. This is so, as suggested in Figure 1-4(B), because this is the period when the world's population will probably spurt to levels almost impossible to imagine—in excess of 10 billion people and possibly as many as 20 billion. Society will have to respond to the needs and aspirations of that huge population more rapidly than new technologies can be invented to solve problems. In short, the needs will have to be answered to a great extent through technologies already developed and through use of resources that have already been identified—the kinds of resources discussed in this book. The challenge posed by the needs and aspirations of 10 billion or more people, and the uneven distribution of the natural resources required to meet the needs, will make the next hundred years the most crucial years the human race has ever faced.

suggestions for further reading

GENERAL

BROBST, D. A., and PRATT, W. P., eds., *United States Mineral Resources.* U.S. Geological Survey Prof. Paper 820, 1973.

CLOUD, P. E., JR., *Resources and Man.* San Francisco: Freeman, 1969.

HOLDGATE, M. W., KASSAG, M., and WHITE, F., eds., *The World Environment 1972–1982. A Report by the United Nations Environment Programme.* Vol. 8 in the Natural Resources and Environmental Series. Dublin: Tycooly International Publishing, Ltd.

LOVERING, T. S., *Minerals in World Affairs.* Englewood Cliffs, N.J.: Prentice-Hall, 1943.

MCDIVITT, J. F., and MANNERS, G., *Minerals and Men.* Baltimore: Johns Hopkins, 1974.

NATIONAL ACADEMY OF SCIENCES, *Mineral Resources and the Environment,* a report prepared by the Committee on Mineral Resources and the Environment, Feb. 1975.

SKINNER, B. J., and TUREKIAN, K. K., *Man and the Ocean.* Englewood Cliffs, N.J.: Prentice-Hall, 1973.

THE STAFF, *Minerals Yearbook, Volumes I and II: Metals, Minerals and Fuels.* U.S. Bureau of Mines, published annually.

FUEL RESOURCES

AVERITT, P., *Coal Resources of the United States, Jan. 1, 1967.* U.S. Geological Survey Bull. 1275.

GRAY, T. J., and GASHUS, D. K., *Tidal Power.* New York: Plenum Press, 1972.

HOBSON, G. D., and TIRATSOO, E. N., *Introduction to Petroleum Geology,* 2nd ed. Beaconsfield, England: Scientific Press, 1981.

LEVORSEN, A. I., *Geology of Petroleum,* 2nd ed. San Francisco: Freeman, 1967.

NATIONAL RESEARCH COUNCIL. *Natural Gas from Unconventional Sources.* Washington, D.C.: National Academy of Sciences, 1976.

PARENT, J. D., *A Survey of United States and Total World Production, Proved Resources, and Remaining Recoverable Resources of Fossil Fuels and Uranium.* Chicago, Ill.: Institute of Gas Technology, 1983.

TIRATSOO, E. N., *Oil Fields of the World.* Beaconsfield, England: Scientific Press, 1973.

WORLD ENERGY COUNCIL, *World Energy Resources, 1985–2020; World Energy Conference.* Guilford, U.K.: IPC Science Tech. Press, 1980.

METAL DEPOSITS

DIXON, C. J., *Atlas of Economic Mineral Deposits.* Ithaca, New York: Cornell Univ. Press, 1979.

DOUGLAS, R. J. W., ed., *Geology and Economic Minerals of Canada.* Economic Geology Report No. 1, Geological Survey of Canada, 1970.

HUTCHINSON, C. S., *Economic Deposits and Their Tectonic Setting.* New York: Springer-Verlag, 1983.

JENSEN, M. L., and BATEMAN, A. M., *Economic Mineral Deposits,* 3rd ed. New York: Wiley, 1979.

MAYNARD, J. B., *Geochemistry of Sedimentary Ore Deposits.* New York: John Wiley and Sons, 1983.

PARK, C. F., Jr., and MACDIARMID, R. A., *Ore Deposits,* 2nd ed. San Francisco: Freeman, 1970.

STANTON, R. L., *Ore Petrology.* New York: McGraw-Hill, 1972.

TITLEY, S. R., *Advances in Geology of the Porphyry Copper Deposits. Southwestern North America.* Tucson: Univ. Arizona Press, 1982.

INDUSTRIAL MINERALS

BATES, R. L., *Geology of the Industrial Rocks and Minerals.* New York: Harper, 1960.

BORCHERT, H. and MUIR, R. O., *Salt Deposits — The Origin, Metamorphism, and Deformation of Evaporites.* Princeton: Van Nostrand, 1964.

GILLSON, J. L., and OTHERS, *Industrial Minerals and Rocks.* Seeley W. Mudd Series, 3rd ed. American Institute of Mining, Metallurgical and Petroleum Engineers, 1960.

WATER RESOURCES

BISWAS, A. K., *History of Hydrology*. Amsterdam: North-Holland Pub. Co., 1970.

DAVIS, S. N., and DEWIEST, R. J. M., *Hydrogeology*. New York: Wiley, 1965.

HUNT, C. A., and GARRELS, R. M., *Water, the Web of Life*. New York: W. W. Norton and Co., 1972.

LEOPOLD, L. B., *Water, A Primer*. San Francisco: W. H. Freeman and Co., 1974.

MCGUINNESS, C. L., *The Role of Ground Water in the National Water Situation*. U.S. Geological Survey, Water-Supply Paper No. 1800, 1963.

U.S. DEPARTMENT OF AGRICULTURE, *Water, The Yearbook of Agriculture*, 1955.

WALTON, W. C., *Groundwater Resource Evaluation*. New York: McGraw-Hill, 1970.

appendix

Table A-1 Units and Their Conversions

MULTIPLES AND SUBMULTIPLES

	Name	Common Prefixes
$10^{12} = 1{,}000{,}000{,}000{,}000$	trillion	
$10^9 = 1{,}000{,}000{,}000$	billion	giga
$10^6 = 1{,}000{,}000$	million	mega
$10^3 = 1{,}000$	thousand	kilo
$10^2 = 100$	hundred	hecto
$10^1 = 10$	ten	deka
$10^{-1} = 0.1$	tenth	deci
$10^{-2} = 0.01$	hundredth	centi
$10^{-3} = 0.001$	thousandth	milli
$10^{-6} = 0.000001$	millionth	micro

CONVERSIONS
BETWEEN COMMON UNITS OF MEASURE
Linear, Area, and Volume Measures

1 kilometer	= 0.6214 mile
1 meter	= 3.281 feet
1 centimeter	= 0.3937 inch
1 square kilometer	= 0.386 square mile
1 square meter	= 10.764 square feet
1 hectare	= 10,000 square meters
	= 2.471 acres
1 square centimeter	= 0.155 square inch
1 cubic kilometer	= 0.240 cubic mile
1 cubic meter	= 35.32 cubic feet
	= 264.2 gallons (U.S.)
1 liter	= 0.264 gallons (U.S.)
1 barrel (oil)	= 42 gallons (U.S.)

Weight and Mass Measures

1 long ton	= 2,240 pounds
1 short ton	= 2,000 pounds

Continued

Table A-1 *(cont.)*

CONVERSIONS
BETWEEN COMMON UNITS OF MEASURE
Linear, Area, and Volume Measures

1 metric ton	= 1,000 kilogram
	= 0.984 long ton
	= 1.102 short tons
1 kilogram	= 2.205 pounds

Energy and Power Measures

1 joule	= 0.239 calorie
1 calorie	= 3.9685×10^{-3} British thermal units (Btu)
1 kilowatt hour	= 10^3 watt hours
	= 3.6×10^6 joules
	= 3,413 Btu
1 watt	= 3.4129 Btu per hour
	= 1.341×10^{-3} horsepower
	= 1 joule per second
	= 14.34 calories per minute

Average equivalents (as used in this book)

1 barrel oil weighs approximately 136.4 kilograms
1 barrel oil is equivalent to approximately 0.22 metric ton coal
1 barrel oil yields approximately 6.0×10^9 joules of energy
1 metric ton of coal yields approximately 27.2×10^9 joules of energy
1 barrel of cement weighs 170.5 kilograms

Table A-2 Principal Ore Minerals and Annual World Production (1982)

I. THE GEOCHEMICALLY ABUNDANT METALS

Element	World Production (metric tons)	Principal Ore Minerals
IRON	788×10^6 (iron ore; average about 60 percent Fe)	Magnetite, Fe_3O_4; Hematite, Fe_2O_3; Goethite, $HFeO_2$; Siderite, $FeCO_3$
ALUMINUM	12.9×10^6	Gibbsite, H_3AlO_3; Diaspore, $HAlO_2$; Boehmite, $HAlO_2$ Kaolinite, $Al_2Si_2O_5(OH)_4$
TITANIUM	4.10×10^6 (ilmenite) 353×10^3 (rutile)	Ilmenite $FeTiO_3$ Rutile, TiO_2
MANGANESE	20.9×10^6 (manganese ore average about 45 percent Mn)	Pyrolusite, MnO_2; Psilomelane, $BaMn_9O_{18}2H_2O$; Cryptomelane, KMn_8O_{16}; Rhodocrosite, $MnCO_3$
MAGNESIUM	274×10^3 (metal) 3.25×10^6 (magnesite)	Magnesite, $MgCO_3$ Dolomite, $CaMg(CO_3)_2$

II. THE GEOCHEMICALLY SCARCE METALS

A. Metals Commonly Forming Sulfide Minerals

Elements	World Production (metric tons)	Other Important Ore Minerals Besides the Native Elements
COPPER	7.78×10^6	Covellite, CuS; Chalcocite, Cu_2S; Digenite, Cu_9S_5; Chalcopyrite, $CuFeS_2$; Bornite, Cu_5FeS_4; Tetrahedrite, $Cu_{12}Sb_4S_{13}$
ZINC	6.16×10^6	Sphalerite, ZnS
LEAD	3.45×10^6	Galena, PbS
NICKEL	520×10^3	Pentlandite $(NiFe)_9S_8$; Garnierite, $H_4Ni_3Si_2O_9$
ANTIMONY	56.6×10^3	Stibnite, Sb_2S_3
MOLYBDENUM	84.4×10^3	Molybdenite, MoS_2
ARSENIC	$> 28 \times 10^3$	Arsenopyrite, $FeAsS$;

Continued

Table A-2 (cont.)

II. THE GEOCHEMICALLY SCARCE METALS

A. Metals Commonly Forming Sulfide Minerals

Elements	World Production (metric tons)	Other Important Ore Minerals Besides the Native Elements
CADMIUM	17×10^3	Orpiment, As_2S_3; Realgar, AsS Substitution for Zn in sphalerite
COBALT	30×10^3	Linnaeite, Co_3S_4; substitution for Fe in pyrite, FeS_2
MERCURY	6.5×10^3	Cinnabar, HgS; Metacinnabar, HgS
SILVER	11.3×10^3	Acanthite, Ag_2S Substitution for Cu and Pb in their common ore minerals.
BISMUTH	$> 2.0 \times 10^3$	Bismuthinite, Bi_2S_3

B. METALS COMMONLY FOUND IN NATIVE FORM

Elements	World Production (metric tons)	Other Important Ore Minerals Besides the Native Elements
GOLD	1275	Calaverite, $AuTe_2$; Krennerite, $(Au,Ag)Te_2$ Sylvanite, $AuAg_3Te_2$
PLATINUM[a]	79.6	Sperrylite, $PtAs_2$; Braggite, (Pd,Pt)S Cooperite, PtS
PALLADIUM[a]	79.6	Arsenopalladinite, Pd_3As; Michenerite, PdBiTe Froodite, $PdBi_2$ Braggite (Pd,Pt)S
RHODIUM[a]	17.9	—
IRIDIUM[a]	11.9	—
RUTHENIUM[a]	8.0	Laurite, RuS_2
OSMIUM[a]	2.0	—

Continued

Table A-2 *(cont.)*

C. METALS COMMONLY FORMING OXYGEN-CONTAINING COMPOUNDS

Elements	World Production (metric tons)	Principal Ore Minerals
BERYLLIUM	109	Beryl, $Be_3Al_2(SiO_3)_6$
CHROMIUM	8.8×10^6	Chromite, $FeCr_2O_4$
NIOBIUM	16.7×10^3	Columbite, $FeNb_2O_6$
		Pyrochlore, $(NaCa)_2Nb_2O_6F$
TANTALUM	420	Tantalite, $FeTa_2O_6$
THORIUM	not reported	Monazite, a rare-earth phosphate-containing thorium by atomic substitution
TIN	238×10^3	Cassiterite, SnO_2
TUNGSTEN	42.7×10^3	Wolframite, $FeWO_4$; Scheelite, $CaWO_4$
URANIUM	not reported	Uraninite (pitchblende), UO_2 Carnotite, $K_2(UO_2)_2 \cdot 3H_2O$
VANADIUM	33.0×10^3	Substituting for Fe in magnetite, Fe_3O_4

[a] Estimated by dividing the platinoid metal production of 199 metric tons in proportion to the relative metal abundances. (After U.S. Bureau of Mines.)

index

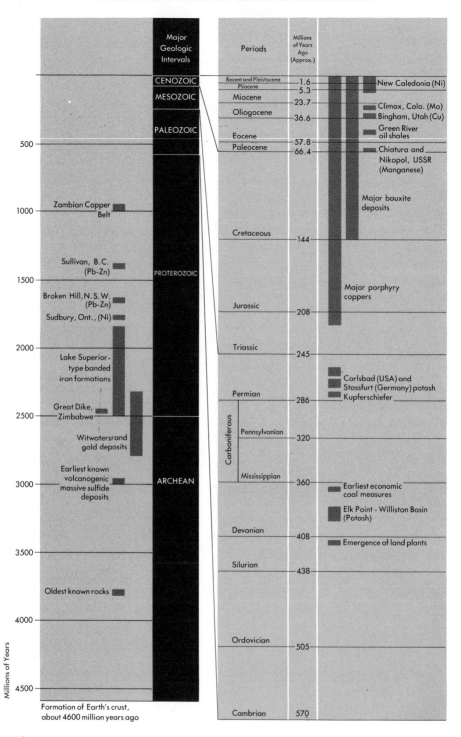

GEOLOGIC TIME SCALE
AND SOME IMPORTANT DATES IN THE FORMATION OF MINERAL RESOURCES